GROW YOUR OWN HERBAL PHARMACY

5 SIMPLE STEPS TO GROW, HARVEST, AND STORE 25 MORE MEDICINAL PLANTS TO CRAFT YOUR OWN NATURAL REMEDIES

JENNI REMPEL

CONTENTS

For my 3 daughters, Kailyn, Meghan and Nicole. I am lucky to have 3 beautiful daughters but even more lucky to have 3 loyal friends. Confident, capable, honourable, & kind. I couldn't be more proud or love you more.

GET YOUR FREE, FULL COLOR PICTURE

Get your free, full color picture of every herb in this book!

Scan this QR code or go to this website:
https://herbalmedicine.homesteadmindset.com/

Many people don't realize this, but it costs more to produce a book with color pictures and I wanted to keep the cost down for you. So please download the "Grow Your Own Herbal Pharmacy Companion Guide" which gives you a full color picture of every herb we discuss in this book. If the QR code doesn't work for you, just go directly to the website. And if for any reason you can't receive the download, please email me at hello@homesteadmindset.com and I would be happy to email this to you.

I hope you enjoy the book love growing herbs in your backyard, patio, or window sill. If you haven't grown an herb before, just start with one and see where it goes.

INTRODUCTION

I woke this morning to hear a news report that there is currently a shortage of amoxicillin, a common antibiotic for treating bacterial infections. Even worse, children's amoxicillin is in the greatest shortage. Just a few months ago, I heard that there was a shortage of Children's Tylenol, all due to supply-chain issues across the country. It made me immediately think of my six grandchildren. I also thought of the many, many parents who may not be able to treat their children's illnesses with the appropriate medications or provide pain relief. What an incredible worry! And if the doctor or pharmacy can't give you what you need, what other choices does a responsible parent have?

Sometimes people assume that growing herbs and making natural remedies is a hobby or a fun lifestyle choice. But in this current climate of shortages and production issues, what if growing your own herbs is your only alternative to safeguard your family's health? I wonder how many people feel comfortable creating natural remedies or know how to do so. I know I didn't until traditional medicines couldn't help me regain health and vitality, and I skeptically sought a natural solution (and was pleasantly surprised!). It has renewed my passion for helping people learn how easy it is to grow an herb and have natural remedies at your fingertips. Not only is it a cost-effective solution, but it may sometimes be the only solution available.

I didn't become a gardener until later in life, and it wasn't a skill that came naturally to me. My love for herbs is certainly not something I have had a life-long passion for. In terms of cooking, I had a small herb garden, but I wouldn't have considered non-culinary uses. Once upon a time, I was probably more of a herbal skeptic than most of you.

Many years ago, my daughter started nagging me about my health. True, it may have been in response to my growing complaints about aches, pains, rashes, and constant bouts of colds and viruses. She had been using herbal remedies and swore by their effectiveness. Listening to this "homesteader" that had emerged from my city-girl roots, I was confident that she was not one to surrender easily.I succumbed and added an aloe vera plant to my windowsill, dubiously watching it for signs of death. Much to my surprise and many "I told you so's" from my daughter, my skin irritation cleared up within miraculous time. It wasn't just the healing that took me by surprise. There was immense satisfaction in walking to my windowsill, taking an aloe vera leaf, and rubbing it straight onto my skin.

One gleeful daughter and one motivated mother later, we decided to look at what other herbal remedies we could put together. Four years after getting my aloe vera plant (which is still alive, I might add), I decided to visit a naturopath which confirmed reinforced to me that pursuing natural remedies made sense.

Regardless of how well we care for ourselves, the natural aging process will impact us. Our bones start to shrink and become less dense, our muscles weaken, and our skin starts to thin and look paler. As we become more forgetful, we walk into the kitchen and wonder why we were going there in the first place. Surely I can't be the only one this happens to!

Though we are far from old, these aches, pains, and concerns lead to more frequent trips to the doctor, and there comes a point when you are sick of feeling like a pin cushion with so many tests. However, ignoring your physical health can have a significant impact on your mental health and quality of life. My good friend recently had a serious health scare, and the impact on her mental health was just as significant as the physical effects until she could get her symptoms under control. It can be scary when you know something is wrong and you are trying to figure out what to do next.

Something as common as backache can impact your ability to work and enjoy social experiences. As much as you try to hide your pain, people start to notice and then treat you like an invalid. The stress of your health and how others perceive you may even cause you to retract a little from society, increasing the risk of stress, anxiety, and depression.

And we aren't talking about old age here! Aging is a gradual process that begins in early adulthood, and the word "old" is now used for those over 70. The signs of natural aging can appear between any of these milestones, depending on our level of self-care. Of course, this doesn't rule out many other health conditions that can creep up on us.

Like me in the past, you might be tempted to rely just on our health care system. The United States is one of the worst performers in global health spending. In 1960, healthcare spending accounted for 5 percent of the total GDP in the US, and in 2020, this hit 20 percent (Morabito, 2022).

So, rising costs in health care lead us to look at other ways to take care of ourselves. According to the typical advice of medical professionals, a healthy balanced diet is crucial. Yeah easier said than done, Doc, with the rising cost of food, not to mention organic food, am I right?

You could buy herbs to make herbal remedies, but this won't eliminate the rising cost of food prices. In 2014, the average unit price of herbs was $15.17, which is expected to rise to $19.87 per unit by 2027 (Statista, 2022).

The future doesn't look too bright when we focus on this side of things. A simple solution for many problems starts with a pack of seeds, which cost a fraction of a package of grown herbs at the store. Plus, with the proper knowledge, you will learn techniques that will allow this one pack of seeds to last decades.

And we aren't just going to do this with one herb. We will do this with 25 herbal plants that often have more than one health benefit. For each of these herbal plants, you will discover how they can improve your well-being and five steps to turning these seeds into practical additions to your medicine cabinet.

With these seeds and techniques, the minute a cold, cough, or other ailment appears, you will have scientifically-proven remedies without needing to drive and spend money in a pharmacy. Opening the back door is enough to find a solution to pain, and even improving our sleep and mood.

This is our third book on the healing power of herbs. *The Homesteader Herbal Handbook,* with the first set of 25 herbs, received so much positive feedback I was blown away. I am happy to report this book was on the Amazon Best Sellers list for over four months! The idea of growing your own medicine motivated me to focus on my second book, *Forget the Pharmacy—Grow Your Own Medicine,* which is still on the Amazon Best Seller List. I think this demonstrates how "hungry" we all are to provide natural, sustainable, and available cures to our families – and I commend each of you for having that goal – especially if you are taking your first baby steps.

The last few months have seen more turmoil in the world, and I want to make a difference with the next volume in our herbal pharmacy journey. This way, more and more people can find the same self-sufficient benefits that I have been able to experience.

Gardening is no longer considered just a hobby for the elderly (sorry Dad), nor is it something only those blessed with a green thumb can do. Growing your own herbs for healing sounds like something you need scientific training for, but we will keep these steps so simple that your family can get involved, stay healthy, and become self-sufficient in terms of health and well-being.

If you have read my previous books, you may know why herbal medicine is making a huge comeback. Let's quickly review why herbal medicine is invaluable but must be respected.

1

WHY YOU SHOULD START MAKING YOUR OWN MEDICINE

Before any growing or healing, there has to be a level of respect for the power of medicinal plants. Like most things, the media loves to focus on the negative and evoke fear in us and often focuses on the potential for using herbs. I firmly believe that herbal plants don't go wrong. But it's easy for people to misuse or misunderstand their power. Nature is wonderful and sucks us in with its beauty, but it doesn't give any warning labels.

A friend had bought a new home with a stunning garden and pointed out her favorite flower as she proudly gave me a tour. As I looked at this shrub with stunning giant flowers, I had a moment of panic. Unbeknownst to her, these were Brugmansia or Angel's Trumpet—one of the deadliest flowers in the world. If you have ever heard of Devil's Breath, the street name for scopolamine, you will know how powerful this hallucinogen is. It wasn't funny at the time, but now we still share an occasional giggle; she could have even gotten in trouble with the law!

Imagine a plant having the ability to enable you to control what others do. The last thing I want to do is alarm you, but a handful of plants are toxic enough to kill. It is estimated 844 plants are toxic to humans (Günthardt et al., 2018). On the other hand, there are anywhere between 50,000 and 80,000 plants that can be used medicinally.

I hope to open your eyes to the power of herbs and how to use them safely. Plants have been used to heal since the dawn of man, although man had no science to back the effectiveness. Today, science is catching up with tradition.

WHAT HISTORY TELLS US ABOUT HERBAL MEDICINE

It isn't easy to pinpoint the time herbs were first used for healing, mainly because there wouldn't have been written documents. The first written records came from clay tablets created by the Sumerians over 5,000 years ago.

The Ancient Egyptians wrote the Ebers Papyrus around 1,500 BCE, and these documents listed some modern favorites like cumin, coriander, and garlic. Other key historical influencers include Ayurveda, the medical system that originated in India and its surrounding areas. Of the 300 herbs, ashwagandha and tulsi are still popular today, not to mention practices like yoga, meditation, and mindfulness. Traditional Chinese Medicine comprises more than 365 herbs, all emphasizing balancing the energies for the best health outcomes. My favorite from this tradition has to be ginger!

In Western Herbal Tradition, Hippocrates was a game changer. He stepped out against contrary beliefs regarding medicine and healing. In 400 BCE, it was common to believe that illness and disease were curses from the gods. Hippocrates drew knowledge from the Egyptians, Indians, and Chinese, and like many Greek physicians of that time, believed that diet, plant and animal-based medicines, and surgery were optimal for health and healing.

The use of herbs continued to gain popularity, and more so once the printing press started to mass produce texts, and these texts were translated. It looked like all was good for using herbal remedies across the globe.

But the plant heroes were soon overshadowed by the practice of "heroic medicines" in the 19th century. Purging, bloodletting, and using toxins such as arsenic and mercury were favored. In 1904, the Council of Medical Education (CME), part of the American Medical Association (AMA), set new standards, placing great competition on those using natural healing methods. Many schools offering homeopathy and naturopathy were forced to drop their courses (Herbal Academy, 2021),

WHAT SCIENCE TELLS US ABOUT HERBAL MEDICINE

Despite influences from "modern" science, herbal medicine wasn't forgotten. A slow revival began as science started to research the benefits of plants and herbs. Today, the World Health Organization (WHO) estimates that 80 percent of the world relies on herbal medicine and, of all the drugs in the world, 25 percent are plant-based (National Health Portal India, 2016).

Before modern technology, we relied on word of mouth, what had worked for the previous generations, and what hadn't. And even in the 20th century, these plants were still effective. The question many of us needed answered was why!

Plants contain phytochemicals that enable them to remain strong and healthy in a particular environment. Humankind and plants have evolved in the same environment, so humans have been able to take advantage of these phytochemicals the same way plants have.

But plants have a very complex set of phytochemicals. Rosehip alone can have approximately 129 chemical compounds. Scientists extract one chemical compound from a plant to make a drug. This one chemical is tested against specific illnesses and diseases and then approved by the Food and Drug Administration (FDA).

So, if you pick a rosehip from your garden, the benefits can be backed by science; in some cases, these specific compounds can be isolated. But 129 (approximately) chemicals will still react with different systems in our body; furthermore, every human body is different. The phytochemicals of each plant will also depend on concentration, where it is grown, and when it is harvested. For this reason, the FDA doesn't regulate many herbal medicines.

At the same time, with numerous phytochemicals comes numerous benefits. With so many vitamins and minerals in plants, you may find that choosing one will help with the aliment you had intended but also improve your health in other ways.

Science and the media also tell us that the future isn't looking bright. Climate change and the consequences of a growing population were already putting pressure on the food supply. In just the last few months, we have seen the impact of war on our food prices. Aside from our health, I believe we must learn how to grow, harvest, and use herbs to prepare us for an uncertain future better. Doing so will help us maintain a healthy diet in the face of rising food prices.

8 REMEDIES TO MAKE FROM WHAT YOU GROW

It might seem like we are jumping ahead of ourselves, but I wanted to look at how to make popular herbal remedies before looking at our 25 herbs. This way, you have a reference to return to when you read how best to use these herbs and spices.

Teas are probably the easiest to prepare and are most often used daily. To make tea, steep your plant parts in hot water for 4 to 5 minutes. Sometimes, you may need to add honey or combine them with other herbs for individual taste.

Infusions

Infusions are a stronger type of tea, typically steeped for 5 to 20 minutes. The extra steeping time allows for more health benefits to be extracted. Infusions can be hot or cold, depending on the herb rather than personal preference. It takes 4 to 8 hours to extract the benefits when making cold infusions.

Decoctions

You must simmer ingredients for 20 to 60 minutes to make a decoction. Decoctions are often better for plant parts that are a little firmer, like roots and stems. Like with teas, the longer you simmer the decoction, the stronger it will be.

Poultices and Compresses

A poultice is used to dress external wounds. You can take a cloth or piece of material and soak it in a tea, infusion, or decoction, then place the poultice on the affected areas. A compress uses fresh parts of the plant wrapped in a cloth and applied to the affected area. You can typically reapply the poultice or compress several times throughout the day.

Tincture

To make a tincture, you need a jar, the herbs of your choice, and alcohol. There is no right or wrong alcohol choice, but many people use vodka because of the lack of flavor. It must be at least 20 percent alcohol by volume (ABV) or 40 proof. The best results come from a 40 to 60 percent ABV (80 to 120 proof), which will extract both water-soluble and alcohol-soluble active ingredients. Fill your jar with herbs, top up the jar with alcohol, and ensure all the herbs are fully covered. Leave in a cool place and shake frequently, preferably every day. Most tinctures are ready in 4 to 6 weeks.

Infused oil or vinegar

The method to infuse oil and vinegar is the same as for tinctures. For vinegar infusions, I like apple cider vinegar for more potent herbs and rice vinegar for milder flavors. There is a wide range of oils, but I try to choose one that is edible to use for cooking and topically. Good choices are coconut oil, sweet almond oil, and olive oil.

A faster method to infuse oil is to use heat. You must create a double-boiler by adding a heat-proof container to a saucepan of hot water. Add your herbs and oil to the heat-proof container and let them simmer for at least 1 hour and up to 5 hours. The oil needs to take on the color and scent of the herbs.

Salves

Once you have your infused oil, use can make a salve for your skin. You will need beeswax; the pellets or shavings are easiest to work with. Add ¼ cup of beeswax to 1 cup of infused oil. Gently melt the beeswax over low heat. When the beeswax has melted, please leave it to cool slightly before transferring it to a tin to cool fully.

Syrups

Again, the beauty of syrups is that you can use any left-over decoction to make a syrup; however, strong decoctions are best. You can use sugar or honey, but I prefer honey because of the additional health benefits. A ratio of 1 cup of decoction to 1 cup of honey will result in the best shelf life for your syrup. If you use less honey, use your syrup sooner.

You will notice that I haven't been exacting with the measurements because it will often depend on your taste buds and how strong you like your herbal remedies. For beginners, experiment with less and gradually add more. This is the safest way to monitor allergic reactions too.

Growing your own herbs (and without fertilizer) will guarantee organic ingredients. For anything you must buy, try to ensure it is organic.

My friend carefully dug out her beautiful yet dangerous plant with no adverse effects. But it is a lesson in knowing your herbs and taking proper precautions. Care has to be taken, so for each of our herbs, I will include potential risks. Nevertheless, if you have any health condition or you are taking any medication, please speak to your doctor before beginning any herbal remedy. The same is said for pregnant and breastfeeding women. Don't worry. Even if you are pregnant, a sprinkle of basil will unlikely harm you, but it is always best to be safe than sorry.

Before we start looking at culinary herbs, let's start our 25 herbs with a plant native to the mountains of North America: arnica.

2

ARNICA

Arnica Montana

Arnica is a perennial flowering plant that grows to about 2 feet high. The flowers are similar to daisies and come in bright orange and yellow. It's actually a member of the sunflower family. It's a great plant to start with because it comes back year after year, and there are no known interactions, making it a safe herb for most people.

WHY ADD ARNICA TO YOUR HERBAL MEDICINE CABINET

Arnica is most often associated with creams and gels to treat aches, pains, bruises, and conditions like arthritis and osteoporosis. Arnica flowers contain helenalin, an active ingredient with anti-inflammatory properties. This is why arnica is good to grow and can treat sports injuries and relieve pain after surgery.

Topically, it can also help reduce the signs of scars and age spots and treat skin conditions like acne, psoriasis, and eczema. It may prevent hair loss, treat dandruff, and strengthen your hair.

5 SIMPLE STEPS TO GROWING ARNICA

Because arnica is a native plant, most gardens will already have the ideal growing conditions for arnica. The plant does well in US hardiness zones 4 to 9 and isn't fussy about soil as long as it's well-drained. This is a good beginner flower for homestead gardeners.

Step 1: Starting Seeds Indoors or Outdoors

While seeds aren't fussy about soil type, you should always start with fresh potting soil so that you don't risk infecting your seeds with viruses or bacteria from older plants. To start seeds indoors, fill starting pots with soil. In the next chapter, we will look at alternatives to save some money and help the environment. Sprinkle the seeds on the soil and then give them a light covering of the soil. Light is necessary for germination, so resist the urge to plant these flower seeds too deeply.

If you start them indoors, plant your seeds a few months before the last expected frost. Or, you can start the seeds in the garden in spring once the last frost has passed. Arnica seeds prefer temperatures of around 55°F (13°C). In either case, use a spray bottle to keep the soil slightly moist.

Step 2: Arnica Plant Needs

Arnica is a slow-growing plant. In the first year, don't expect much growth; you only need to keep an eye on the soil moisture. Once the seedlings are a few inches tall, you can gently dig up the plants and move them so that they are around 12 inches apart. If you have started them in containers, don't panic about transplanting them, as you can leave them for up to a year before moving to your garden.

When choosing a permanent home for arnica, look for an area with full sun, meaning the site should have more than 6 hours of sunlight a day. Some varieties can handle partial shade, so check the packet instructions for light requirements. Don't worry if your arnica plant seems to die when winter comes. You can cut it right back to the ground. It is dormant in winter and will bounce back to life in spring.

Step 3: Faster Ways to Grow Arnica

Instead of growing arnica from the seeds, you can also propagate the plant from a cutting or the roots. The rhizomatic roots will be strong enough to divide in the second year of growth. In the early spring, dig around the base of the plant to loosen the soil, gently lift the plant out of the soil, digging the soil away if need be. Cut the root ball in half and replant the separate plants with a pair of sharp scissors.

Step 4: Harvesting Arnica Flowers and Roots

There are two harvesting options. First of all, you can harvest only the flowers. Pick them individually when the center florets are open. Instead of having mini balls in the middle of the flower, you will see mini flowers. It's usually best to harvest flowers in the morning after the dew has dried but before the full sun is on them, as this is when they have the most volatile oils.

Be careful if you have any open wounds on your skin. The irony of this plant is that although it can help with several skin conditions, the oil from freshly picked flowers can be irritating.

The second method is to dig up the entire plant, roots and all. The roots are less commonly used but still have medicinal benefits. Brush the roots off and cut away the stems. Rinse them under running water and pat them dry with a paper towel.

Step 5: Long-Term Storage for Arnica

To dry the flowers, you can pick the heads off the stems and spread them on a rack or piece of paper. Leave the flowers in a warm, dry area with plenty of airflow. The flowers take a few days to dry. Take one of the flowers and see if it crumbles and flakes between your fingers. If it doesn't crumble, leave them for a couple more days.

Arnica roots are very fine and only take a few days to 1 week to dry completely, and the roots will snap when dried correctly. Resist the temptation to store the flowers or roots before they are fully dried out. If you store them too soon, any remaining moisture may cause mold to grow in the airtight containers, which can ruin your harvest.

HOW TO USE YOUR ARNICA FLOWERS AND ROOTS

For topical uses, try to infuse oils or make a salve. Add shea butter to your infused oil and beeswax to make a cream. For the skin and hair, you can also make a decoction. Once you know that your skin isn't irritated by arnica flowers, you can rub the fresh flowers onto the affected area. It's best not to do this if the skin is broken.

The roots can be used for an oil infusion, fresh or dried. If you want to make a tea or tincture out of arnica flowers and roots, make the tea weak and dilute the tincture in water or other liquids. Arnica flowers can be poisonous in large doses but are generally safe when diluted! Don't take arnica if there are any signs of shortness of breath, increased heart rate, rashes, diarrhea, or vomiting.

Next, we'll explore the wonderful benefits of a culinary herb that sits right outside my kitchen window, prized for both its versatility in cooking an dits medicinal uses.

3

BASIL

Ocimum Basilicum

Basil is one of the kindest herbs for new homesteaders. Because it is an annual, meaning its lifecycle lasts one year, it grows incredibly quickly. It can be grown indoors or outdoors, and as a culinary herb, it's so versatile.

Basil is a member of the mint family, and there are various types of basil you can grow. African Blue basil has purple flowers and green and purple leaves, giving you a nice peppery flavor. The Cinnamon basil and Lemon basil produce flavors that match their names. Holy basil, also known as Tulsi, is a versatile herb that can be used for cooking but is more popular for its medicinal properties and revered as a sacred plant in Ayurvedic medicine.

WHY BASIL SHOULD BE THE FIRST CULINARY HERB TO GROW

One thing you will read a lot about in this book is antioxidants. Antioxidants are substances that are best found in plant-based foods. Popular antioxidants we have all heard of are vitamins C, and E. Antioxidants are vital for helping to protect the body from free radicals, molecules that damage our cells. Damaged cells can increase your risk of diseases such as arthritis, diabetes, cancer, and heart disease.

Some free radicals occur naturally in the body; others come from environmental factors like smoke, pollution, and radiation. When free radicals and antioxidants are imbalanced, oxidative stress occurs. By increasing the intake of antioxidants, our bodies are in a healthy position to fight free radicals.

Basil contains the antioxidants lutein, zeaxanthin, beta-carotene, and beta-cryptoxanthin. It also contains calcium, vitamins A and K, manganese, magnesium, iron, zinc, and potassium.

These nutrients can help regulate blood sugar and may even be able to treat high blood sugar levels. Eugenol in basil can block calcium channels and help lower blood pressure, while magnesium improves blood flow. This may help lower cholesterol and reduce the risk of heart disease. Eugenol, linalool, and citronellol may also reduce inflammation in the body. You might think that inflammation is related to muscles and injuries, but these active ingredients can also reduce inflammation caused by arthritis, heart disease, and some bowel problems.

BASIL FOR BEGINNER HOMESTEADERS

Despite being native to southern Asia, it takes little effort to grow your own basil. If you are planning to grow basil indoors, you can start your seeds any time of year. If you are planting outdoors, begin in the early spring.

Step 1: Planting Basil Seeds

Even for outdoor growing, there are two ways to start basil seeds, and this applies to most seeds too. You can start your basil indoors 4 to 8 weeks before the last frost or sow directly into a container outside once the last frost has passed. Basil is a tender plant and doesn't like the cold.

Start with fresh potting soil in a starter pot. While you can purchase starter pots, I prefer to use alternatives such as recycled yogurt containers or even toilet paper rolls and other cardboard materials, as they will eventually break down and enrich the soil with nutrients. It's a small way to help the environment.Place a few seeds about ¼ of an inch below the soil surface. Then, with a spray, moisten the soil—Basil seeds like humidity to germinate, so it will help if you cover the seeds in plastic wrap. The ideal location is around 70°F. Within 7 to 10 days, your basil should start to shoot. Don't panic if there is no sign of life on day ten. You may need a couple more days.

Step 2: Caring for Your Basil Plant

Once your seedlings have appeared, you can remove the plastic. Now you can leave your starter trays in a sunny area and continue to spray with a mister to keep the soil moist. The leaves you see on the plant at this stage aren't true leaves. Think of them like milk teeth on a child! They can't perform photosynthesis and create their own food. Therefore, before we transplant the seedlings, you should always ensure there are true leaves on the stem. True leaves look like adult leaves but are smaller and tend to take 1 to 3 weeks to appear.

To transplant the seedlings, gently remove them from the starting pots and place them in a larger container with fresh soil. Seedlings, especially the root structures, are very delicate. This is why I prefer using cardboard to start seeds. You can lift the cardboard with the seedling and transplant the whole plant without risking the structure.

When a basil plant has three sets of leaves, it is ready to move outdoors gradually. This process is called hardening off. Leave the plant outside for 1 hour in a sunny spot. Increase the amount of time it stays outside. Once the outdoor temperature is consistently above 70°F, they will be safe outside. Your basil plant will love you if you provide it with 6 to 8 hours of sunlight daily.

Basil likes to be kept moist, so regular water ensures moisture gets down to the roots is essential. Aim for around an inch of water weekly, but this may need to increase in the summer months.

Once more leaves come through, pinch the top sets to keep the basil plant healthy and encourage the growth of abundant leaves. Because it's tender, you only need your nails to pinch off the leaves.

Step 3: Propagating Basil

If you want to grow another basil plant from the one you have, cut a stem that is approximately 4 inches long. Be sure to cut below the leaf node, the little "joint" where the leaf meets the stem. Place the stem in a glass of water on a windowsill and change the water every few days. The cutting will have around 2 inches long roots within one week or two. This is the time to transplant the cutting to a container with soil.

Step 4: How to Harvest Basil

Basil can be harvested as needed by pinching off a few leaves. You should also aim to have a bigger harvest once a month. This way, the plant will continue producing more leaves throughout the season. Cut about ⅓ of the stems monthly for a healthy plant and plenty of new growth.

Step 5: The Best Ways to Store Basil

Fresh basil will last for one week or two, either in a glass of water on your kitchen counter or wrapped in a paper towel and then in a plastic bag in the fridge. You might want to freeze basil for a larger harvest, but you should definitely blanch it first. Pull the leaves off the stem and add them to a colander. Dip the colander into boiling water, ensuring all the leaves are soaked, and then straight into a bowl of ice water. This will help preserve the color and flavor.

From there, you can pat the leaves dry and freeze them in a bag or chop them and add them to ice cube trays with water or your favorite cooking oil. Frozen basil will be good for up to 3 months.

It is best to use fresh basil, so we will look at drying techniques for more appropriate herbs. When dried, basil tends to lose a lot of the health benefits.

FLAVOR FOR MORE THAN PIZZA AND PASTA

Having ample basil on your doorstep will encourage you to use this herb for more than your traditional Italian meals. Blend leaves into a purée and add to soups and sauces, and don't forget to add some leaves to a salad for more flavor.

For medicinal uses, steep 5 or 6 leaves in hot water for around 5 minutes (more leaves for longer will strengthen the tea). The tea may help with digestive problems and can ease a sore throat with a little bit of honey. If you feel congested, take advantage of the steam from the tea to inhale.

Basil tea may also work for tension headaches, but if you have migraines, chewing on a basil leaf may be more effective. If you have an insect bite or sting, crush some leaves and rub them over the affected area.

As basil is an annual, saving some of the seeds once the plant has flowered is a good idea. When flowers turn brown, cut them off and pop them in a brown paper bag. Leave the flower heads dry for a few days, then shake the bag well. The flower heads will come apart, and you will see tiny black seeds. Store them in an airtight container away from direct sunlight until the next spring.

Many of the techniques you have learned in this chapter will be relevant to other herbs, especially culinary ones. Until then, we will move on to our second medicinal plant, a citrus fruit that gives Earl Grey its distinctive flavor.

4

BERGAMOT

Bergamot – Citrus Fruit: Citrus Bergamia
Bergamot – Wild: Monarda Fistulosa

There are two types of bergamot, so as a bonus, I have included information about both the citrus fruit and wild bergamot. Wild bergamot is native to North America. It's a perennial plant with purple, pink, or white flower clusters. Wild bergamot can grow 2 to 5 feet, making it one of the tallest of the mint family.

The citrus fruit is native to Asia, but Southern Italy grows much of the world's bergamot supply. Fruits appear from October to March and are normally the size of a small orange, though the taste is much more sour. The fruit can be yellow or orange.

HOW THE TWO BERGAMOTS IMPROVE HEALTH

With the citrus fruit, the essential oils can improve your mood, reducing the symptoms of stress and anxiety, even as much as diazepam does. Limonene, linalyl acetate, and linalool in these fruits have anti-inflammatory properties and may help reduce pain. The phytochemical naringin may help with weight loss. With antiseptic, anti-microbial, and antibacterial properties, bergamot can help your skin in plenty of ways.

Wild bergamot has high amounts of thymol. Native Americans taught the settlers how to use wild bergamot to treat coughs and colds, sore throats, nausea, gas, colic, and fever because of the antiseptic and antibacterial properties. Traditionally, it has also been used for its calming effects.

WHICH IS BEST FOR YOU TO GROW

First, consider the space you have. The citrus plant can grow to over 6 feet. Because of its native origins, it also prefers temperatures over 60°F. If your climate drops below this temperature, you will need to be able to move the plant indoors. Like other mints, wild bergamot tends to spread, so it's wise to grow it in a container.

Step 1: Getting Bergamot Started

With citrus bergamot seeds, plan to plant the seeds in spring, but never later than summer. Moisten the potting soil first and check that your container has holes in the bottom to ensure the soil drains well. Place the seeds 1 inch under the soil and leave the container in full sun.

Growing wild bergamot from seeds is as simple as growing any culinary herb. Place the seeds about ¼ inch under the soil surface and keep the soil slightly moist with a spray. Start the seeds indoors 6 to 8 weeks before the last frost. If you want to plant the seeds outdoors, you can plant them when there is still a light frost, but the seeds prefer temperatures of 60°F to 70°F. It will take between 10 and 40 days for the seeds to sprout, depending on the temperature.

Step 2: Growing Needs of Bergamot

Aside from the temperature, bergamot doesn't need a great deal of care. It can tolerate periods of drought, but younger plants, especially those in a container, will need more regular watering. Like many other citrus fruits, the soil needs plenty of nutrients, so it's a good idea to add compost during the spring and summer months when the flowers are turning into fruit. Keep your wild bergamot well-watered. The flowers you don't harvest should be deadheaded (pinched off) to ensure the plant's energy goes to keeping it healthy and producing new flowers. If you see the leaves at the bottom of the stem turning yellow, cut the stems back.

Prune the plant at the end of winter. Cut back any dead branches, branches that cross over others, and those that are dense so that air can flow through.

Keep your wild bergamot well-watered. The flowers you don't harvest should be deadheaded (pinched off) to ensure the plant's energy goes to keeping it healthy and producing new flowers. If you see the leaves at the bottom of the stem turning yellow, cut the stems back.

Step 3: How to Increase Your Bergamot Yield

If you want to grow additional bergamot plants for fruit, find a 6-inch cutting. Choose one of the healthy young tips with no fruit or flowers growing. This way, the plant's energy will form new roots. There should be at least 2 or 3 nodes on the stem. These nodes contain the cells that are needed for roots. Plant the cutting straight into a starter pot with fresh soil.

To promote new growth and the added bonus of gaining a second plant, it's recommended to separate the Bergamot plant once every three years. To do this, remove the entire plant from its container and split it down the center. If you notice that the center of the plant is starting to die in the spring, this is a clear indication that it's time to divide it. Once you've separated the plant into two parts, replant each part in a container with fresh soil. It's important to ensure that there's plenty of air circulation for the new plants to thrive.

Step 4: Ways to Harvest Bergamot

Bergamot fruit ripens in winter, so keep an eye on the fruit from November onward. Once the fruit turns yellow, they are ready to be harvested by carefully picking them off the branches.

Wild bergamot can be harvested by cutting the whole stem a few inches from the ground. If you want to harvest the seeds, you need to wait until the seeds are black/brown, and you can use the paper bag trick to save some seeds for another growing season.

Step 5: Storing Bergamot for Long-Term Use

The only way to store your harvested bergamot fruit is in the fridge. They will stay fresh for up to 2 weeks. We will explore long-term preservation in the next section.

Whole stems of wild bergamot can be dried by bundling them and hanging them upside down in a place with good air circulation. It can take up to 2 weeks for them to fully dry. You can also separate the plant parts and dry them in a dehydrator or oven on the lowest heat setting. When fully dry, crush the leaves in your fingers and store them in paper bags. Depending on your uses, you can keep the dried flower heads together or separately.

USES FOR BERGAMOT

Bergamot can be a versatile ingredient in cooking and personal care. It can be used in recipes that call for oranges or lemons. For instance, you can add fresh fruit slices to hot water for tea or even to cold water for a new and refreshing flavor. Grating the citrus fruit into baked goods, especially cookies, can add a delightful taste as well. Additionally, you can use the fruit peel to infuse oil for hair and skin care.

Both types of bergamot can also be made into a salve using oil infusions.The leaves, flowers, and stalks of the plant are all edible, providing a range of flavor possibilities. Wild bergamot is highly aromatic, so if you want to use it to scent your home, it's best to use it sparingly. Leaves and flowers can be used in teas and raw in salads. They can also be added to baked goods, marinades, and sauces for extra spice. Use the leaves like you would oregano, dried or fresh. You could also try infusing vinegar with the flowers.

Bergamot is the latest addition to my garden, so I promise I will let you know how my marmalade turns out! Until then, we will continue with an extremely popular culinary spice that you might not have considered growing, but the next chapter will hopefully inspire you to try.

5

CINNAMON

Cinnamomum Verum

There are two relationships with cinnamon: love and hate. Not everyone can get their palate around the spicy citrus flavors; others can't get enough of it. If you love it, you will love it even more after this chapter. If you hate it, I hope the health benefits will tempt you.

YOUR HEART WILL THANK YOU FOR CINNAMON

What makes cinnamon so special is the cinnamaldehyde. Not only does it give the bark of the plant its pungent smell, but it also provides many positive health benefits. For the heart, cinnamon can reduce blood pressure, blood sugar, and bad cholesterol, all of which are risk factors for heart disease. Cinnamaldehyde has antifungal and antibacterial properties.

More research needs to be done, but cinnamon may also protect neurons in the brain and may be able to help neurodegenerative diseases such as Alzheimer's and Parkinson's diseases.

Cinnamon has such high levels of antioxidants that it can be used as a natural food preservative. The antioxidants protect cells from free radicals and have anti-inflammatory properties. Although more research needs to be done, it may also have anti-cancer effects.

HOW TO GROW THIS TROPICAL PLANT AND HARVEST THE BARK

To grow healthy cinnamon, you will need to mimic the native conditions. The ideal temperature for cinnamon is around 80°F and never below 40°F. The plant doesn't like dry climates. It will also grow in containers indoors.

Step 1: Wait for the Sun

If you are planting from the seed, plant them about ½ an inch into fresh soil. If you are planting directly outside, you must wait until spring and plant in a spot in your garden that receives around 12 hours of sunlight a day. If you want to start the seeds indoors, plant them 170 to 180 days before spring. It can take up to 21 days for the seeds to sprout.

If you find a young plant at a nursery, transplant it into a permanent container or the ground again in spring. Be sure to dig a hole bigger than the container that it comes in and add a little compost to the hole before planting.

Step 2: Spritz Away

As seedlings, the best way to water cinnamon is through generous spraying to keep the top layer of soil moist. Once those true leaves come through, it's time to transplant them to their permanent home. Again, keep spritzing to keep the soil moist. If you plan to keep your plant indoors, spritzing is still the best way to water it. For outdoor plants, try to mimic tropical conditions. Once the top few inches of soil are dry, give the plant a decent watering.

Step 3: Patience With Cuttings

It can take several months for a cutting to develop roots, but that's not to say it isn't worth it. Take a cutting around 6 inches long, and remove the lower leaves. Add soggy soil to a container and ensure the cutting is planted deep enough so that it is sturdy.

Step 4: How Long Until Harvest?

It will take two or three years to harvest cinnamon, and it is so much fun doing it because it's easier than you think. Cut off a few branches and scrape off the outer bark. You will start to see a yellow-orange layer. You want to peel strips of this layer, either with a knife or a paint scraper. Peel until you see the lighter core of the branch. You can do this every two years.

Step 5: Two Years' Worth of Cinnamon

Leave your harvested cinnamon to dry for about one week. During this time, you will see the bark start to curl as you see it in the shops. You can either store the sticks whole or grind them into a powder—with enough harvest, you can have a bit of both. Stored in an airtight container, cinnamon should last for two years.

GETTING CREATIVE WITH CINNAMON

Cinnamon works wonders in pastry recipes, especially paired with apples and sultanas. Add one or two cinnamon sticks to 8 cups of water and boil for 2 or 3 minutes to make cinnamon tea. Daily cinnamon tea can help with urinary tract infections, period pain, indigestion, arthritis pain, cold, and flu, and improve circulation.

Add 1 part of ground cinnamon to 3 parts of honey for a face mask. Add an equal amount of cinnamon powder to your conditioner and leave it on your hair overnight if you want lighter hair. Finally, if you suffer from bad breath, try chewing on a bit of cinnamon stick.

From the exotic to a humble little flower, that may have been one of the first plants we learned to identify at a young age. Despite old wives' tales, our next plant is rarely appreciated for its health benefits, but it should be!

WOULD YOU TAKE 60 SECONDS AND LEAVE ME A REVIEW?

Would you take 60 seconds to leave me a review on Amazon? Just scan the QR code and it will take you to the right place to share your opinion of this book.

Many of us are experiencing increasing costs in all areas of our life, and even more of us are suffering from the stressful lives we lead. By sharing your opinions, others get to see that they have the means to take control of their own health and well-being and that of their families.

Your reviews help this book become more visible and that means others will have a chance to see it also.

Your support means to much – Thank you!

Jenni

6

DANDELION

TARAXACUM OFFICINALE

Taraxacum Officinale

Dandelions are often seen as a weed because of their ability to spread so quickly. Amazingly, the average flower has between 150 and 200 seeds, and there can be ten flowers per plant. Long before their unfortunate reputation, it is thought that dandelions were carried on the Mayflower to North America from Eurasia because of their medicinal benefits.

There is no need to worry. These meadow herbs are only considered invasive in Alaska and Oregon (James River Association, 2021). Aside from their medicinal benefits, dandelions are an excellent addition to any garden for beneficial pollinators like bees.

TRADITIONAL AND MODERN USES OF DANDELION

Native Americans would boil dandelion roots and leaves to treat kidney and liver problems, inflammation, heartburn, and skin problems. The Chinese have used this herb for stomach problems but, interestingly, for breast problems, specifically inflammation and a lack of milk flow. In Europe, people used it for eye problems, fever, and even diabetes.

Dandelion is full of vitamins A, B, C, and D and active ingredients such as araxacin, taraxacerin, inulin, and levulin. So far, most studies have been on animals, but the results are promising and match many traditional uses. Dandelion may help with liver disease, joint inflammation, and diabetes and boost the immune system. Because of the antioxidants, the plant could help with oxidative stress and, more specifically, possibly help fight prostate cancer.

Dandelion is also a strong diuretic. A diuretic causes the body to produce more urine, removing excess liquid from the body. A healthy urinary system is essential to remove toxins and waste from your body.

5 STEPS TO GROW DANDELIONS IF THEY DON'T POP UP ON YOUR LAWN

The problem with dandelions is that they often appear in your lawn, and of course, you can harvest them before you mow the lawn. Still, having a dedicated area or container for medicinal use and control is often more practical!

Step 1: It's Not Hard to Find Seeds

It seems ironic to advise on how to grow dandelions since many of us spend the summer trying to rid our yards of them. Like many seeds, you should plant dandelion seeds around six weeks before the last frost, and they only need to be planted around ¼ of an inch under the soil surface. This depth will help the sunlight reach the seeds for germination; dandelion seeds can tolerate lower soil temperatures of about 50°F even though they prefer the temperatures to be slightly warmer. It can take 10 to 14 days to see the seeds sprout, but if the soil temperature is lower, don't worry if this takes a little longer.

Step 2: Caring for This Simple Meadow Herb

As you might imagine, dandelions don't need a lot of care. Check the soil every few days, and if the topsoil feels dry, water them. The most important thing is to thin the plants once they start growing. A dandelion plant can grow to be 6 inches tall and wide. If they aren't transplanted to their final home with a distance of at least 6 inches, there might not be enough air circulation for healthy growth.

Step 3: In Case You Need to Propagate Dandelion

A dandelion plant can live for anywhere from 5 to 10 years, and because they self-pollinate, it's unlikely you will need to do anything for a continuous source of plant parts. The root system of dandelions has a strong taproot and just a few feeder roots that spread horizontally. A new plant can grow even if you dig up the taproot and leave the feeder roots.

Step 4: Time for Harvest

The roots can be harvested at any time of the year, but it's said that harvesting roots in the fall are best for medicinal uses. To gather the flowers, the best time is a sunny day in the early afternoon. All the dew will have dried, and the flowerheads will be fully open. You can pinch the flowerheads off or cut the stem close to the ground to use more plant parts.

Step 5: Storing Your Dandelions

The parts can be kept in a plastic bag or wrapped in a damp paper towel in the fridge if you plan to use your harvest in the following days. You can air-dry the flowerheads by leaving them in the sun for 3 or 4 days until completely dry. The leaves will take around the same time. To test the leaves, make sure they snap in your fingers. The leaves also do quite well frozen, but, like basil, it's best to blanch them first. If you aren't using your dandelions fresh, they can be hung in a cool, dry place with good airflow. It can take a couple of weeks for the roots to become brittle.

WHAT TO DO WITH ALL THE DANDELION PARTS

If you have harvested young leaves, they make a great salad. Older leaves may taste bitter, so they are best for cooking. You can boil the leaves for around 5 minutes and then sauté them with oil and garlic! Use the petals in baking and even cooking. You can add them to cakes, bread, cookies, hamburgers, and quiches.

You can make the fresh roots into tea. If you have dried them, they can be boiled or ground into a powder and added to hot water. My favorite use for the flowerheads is to infuse the oil. The oil can be used for cooking, or you can add a few drops to your bath.

Dandelions are a member of the daisy family, so if you know you are allergic to any member of the daisy family, you should avoid using dandelions. The same can be said for marigolds, chamomile, feverfew, and yarrow.

As many of you probably do, I remember my grandparents telling me not to pick dandelions because they make you wet the bed. What used to be an old wives' tale for me made sense considering the diuretic powers of this herb.

Next, we will go back to our culinary herbs. Dill is most commonly found as a feathery green herb. However, homesteading is all about leaving nothing to waste, so we will also look at dill as a spice.

7

DILL

Anethum Graveolens

Dill is another good choice for homestead gardeners because, like basil, it's easy to grow. Typically, it's an annual herb, but given the right conditions, it can be grown as a biennial. Dill is a member of the parsley and celery family, but they look very different. The dill plant has ferny foliage that tastes sweet, fresh, and somewhat grassy while also looking attractive.

11 HEALTH BENEFITS DILL CAN OFFER

Dill gets its health benefits from monoterpenes such as limonene and carvone. There are several flavonoids that have antioxidant properties. Then there are good amounts of vitamins A and C and trace amounts of iron, manganese, and folate.

The essential oils in dill can help with insomnia and relaxation. Some calcium in dill may strengthen bones and help protect against diseases like osteoporosis. It may help manage diabetes, but this area needs more research on humans to verify. Dill can help ease gas and diarrhea and even calm the hiccups. Because of its antimicrobial properties, dill can help boost the immune system and help the skin heal. The flavonoids and monoterpenes in dill can help the respiratory system, whether with coughs and colds or allergies. It may relieve as an anti-inflammatory and improve your dental health. Finally, some women use dill to regulate their periods!

FROM PLANTING TO STORING DILL

Dill is not a plant that transplants well because of the taproot it produces. For this reason, it's best to plant your dill directly into its permanent home. If you live in warmer climates, this can be outside in your soil. Dill will grow indoors, too, as long as there is plenty of light.

Step 1: Consecutive Planting

To get a longer harvest, it's a good idea to space out dill planting. You will get a single large crop if you plant all of your seeds at once. But if you plant several seeds each week, you will have weeks of harvest. Like most culinary herbs, the seeds only need to be planted ¼ of an inch under the soil surface when the temperatures are around 70°F. Sow the seeds around 10 to 12 inches apart for sufficient space. It takes about 10 to 12 days to see signs of sprouting.

Step 2: Don't Fuss Over Dill

Really, the only thing you need to do is ensure your dill plant gets full sun (over 6 hours a day) and that the soil is kept moist. You might need to increase the amount of water as the plant is growing. As the leaves start to grow, they may need some protection from the wind.

Step 3: To Propagate or Not to Propagate

The answer here is that if you haven't had a great success rate with seed germination, you might want to grow new plants from a cutting. In summer, dill will flower, and if these yellow flowers are left untouched, and the soil is not disturbed, dill will likely reappear in the following spring.

To grow a new plant from a cutting, choose an older stem because it will be stronger. Cut a stem so that you have approximately 4 inches. Cut the stem at an angle so that more water can be absorbed. Pop this cutting in a glass of water, and you should see new roots sprouting in less than one week. If the water starts to discolor, change the water. After 2 to 3 weeks, there should be enough root growth to transplant it.

Step 4: Count Your Dill Leaves to Know When to Harvest

I have always been a fan of doing the taste test before harvesting. You should harvest the older leaves first, but if you leave the leaves for too long, they can taste bitter. A promising sign is when the stem has 4 or 5 leaves before the plant flowers. These leaves can be pinched off or cut with scissors. For a larger harvest, cut the entire stem.

Dill attracts wasps, and although you may think you don't want wasps in your garden, they kill off some pesky insects. Another benefit of leaving some flowers is that you can harvest the seeds for dill spice! Put some flowerheads in a paper bag, leave them to dry for one week, and shake the bag to separate the seeds from the flowerheads.

Step 5: Fresh, Frozen, or Dried Dill?

To keep your dill leaves fresh in the fridge, wash them off, pat them dry, and place them in a damp paper towel and then in an airtight bag or container. For longer storage, freeze dill for up to a few months. The ice cube tray trick with water or oil is perfect.

Dill isn't a moisture-retaining herb which makes it perfect for drying. The flavors become more concentrated when dry, so you can use less. It's easy to dry the leaves on the stem in bundles. You will know they are completely dry when the leaves snap.

HOW TO USE DILL AND WHO SHOULDN'T USE IT

Add your fresh or dried dill seeds, whole or crushed, into bread, soups, and with different vegetables. Leaves can be used with fish, eggs, poultry, and salads. If you are using fresh dill, add it right at the end.

Other herbal remedies include teas with around two teaspoons of crushed dill in a cup of boiling water, more if your tastebuds fancy it. A dill tincture is one of the best ways to treat various health conditions.

If you have issues with your blood sugar levels, take care with dill in case medicinal amounts of dill cause blood sugar to drop too far. If you are pregnant, you should also take care of medicinal amounts. Dill can cause your period to start, so if you are pregnant, this could cause a miscarriage.

Potato salad is a great side dish, and I like adding a bit of garlic to liven things up. When you harvest dill at the right time, your potato salad can become the star of the meal.

As parents, the worst time of the year is when school starts, and all those viruses start spreading like wildfire. Those chest rubs are a blessing in disguise, but why buy them when you can make your own?

8

EUCALYPTUS

Eucalyptus Globulus

I'm fairly sure I'm not the only one who thinks of eucalyptus and cute koalas munching on leaves. This is a perfect example of how animals and plants have evolved, and Koalas are smart enough to know how to stay healthy.

Eucalyptus is most commonly used to treat the symptoms of colds and flu, but you can probably guess that this plant has more potential benefits. It thrives in US hardiness zones 8 to 11, so it's another that prefers the warmer side of life. If you want to grow eucalyptus indoors, it's best to choose a shrub variety and not a tree variety!

WHY ADD A EUCALYPTUS PLANT TO YOUR HOMESTEAD ENVIRONMENT

Eucalyptus leaves contain high levels of antioxidants, particularly flavonoids, which come in different forms like catechins, isorhamnetin, luteolin, and kaempferol. This makes eucalyptus a useful plant for safeguarding the body against diseases like heart disease, dementia, and certain cancers. Eucalyptus is also used to alleviate cold symptoms due to its anti-inflammatory properties, which help to reduce mucus and congestion. Additionally, it may assist in bronchi expansion, which could help with asthma. These anti-inflammatory properties may also provide pain relief.

There are good reasons to use eucalyptus topically too. The leaf extract could help with dry skin, dandruff, dermatitis, and psoriasis. Inhaling eucalyptus can reduce blood pressure and stress. As a mouthwash, the compounds can reduce bacteria in the mouth that may lead to cavities and gum disease. If that's not enough, the eucalyptol in the oil helps keep the insects at bay.

REQUIREMENTS FOR EUCALYPTUS

Finding eucalyptus plants in nurseries is not always easy, so starting from seed is often the only option. Even then, you may have to buy your seeds online because the wildfires in Australia a couple of years ago led to a seed shortage.

Step 1: Start Eucalyptus Seeds Indoors

Starting your seeds indoors gives them the best chance of germination, and if you have a heat mat, this can help the process. Check the variety of eucalyptus before you do anything. Some types need a period of cold stratification. This means they must be mixed and added to damp soil in a plastic bag and kept in the fridge for six weeks, mimicking nature.

Choose small containers if you plan on transplanting the seedlings, or they can go straight into a larger container. The seeds only need a light layer of soil on top of them, and you should either spray them or water them from the bottom. They aren't keen on soggy soil. The seeds will germinate in 14 to 21 days but should remain indoors for 10 to 12 weeks.

Step 2: When to Move Eucalyptus Outdoors

When your seedlings reach 4 to 6 inches in height, they can be transplanted and moved outdoors. Don't forget to harden them off by slowly introducing them to the outdoor climate. Don't expect your plants to do much in the first few weeks. Then all of a sudden, you will noticed they will start to grow very quickly.

Eucalyptus has a unique advantage with its waxy leaf coating that protects against pests and aids in water retention. Keep an eye on the soil to ensure it doesn't try out too much, but regular watering shouldn't be necessary unless there is a prolonged lack of rain.

Step 3: Why You Should Propagate This Plant

Depending on the conditions and variety, some eucalyptus plants are grown annually. For this reason, I like to take a cutting during the summer months to keep an indoor plant over winter, ready for the following spring. Choose a mature shoot that is 4 inches long and has at least one budding leaf.

Place the cutting in a container with fresh potting soil. The container needs a hole in the bottom to absorb water from a saucer. Cover the container in a plastic bag and leave it in a warm place. The ideal temperature is between 80°F to 90°F, and in the four weeks it takes for the roots to establish, ensure the saucer has water.

Step 4: How to Harvest the Leaves

Timing is everything when it comes to harvesting eucalyptus leaves. Fall to early winter is ideal because you don't want them to experience a hard frost, but you don't want to harvest too early because the leaves might wilt. The leaves should feel firm, almost leathery, rather than soft. Cut entire stems, starting with the longest ones.

Step 5: The Best Ways to Keep Eucalyptus

Eucalyptus can stay fresh anywhere from 2 weeks to 2 months. Just place it in a jar of water or add it to other flower arrangements. For long-term preservation, hang the stems in bundles and let them dry in an area without direct sunlight. It will take 2 to 6 weeks for this. Then you can pick the leaves off the stem and store them in an airtight container.

For topical use and years of preservation, you can use vegetable glycerin. Boil 2 cups of water with 1 cup of vegetable glycerin. Once the liquid has cooled, add it to a vase and place the stems in. After 2 to 6 weeks, the leaves will darken and become soft. Now they are ready to be stored in an airtight container.

USES OF AND CARE WITH EUCALYPTUS

One of my favorite uses of eucalyptus is to hang some of the stems in the shower for wonderful steam inhalation. Depending on the shower's use, they can last up to 2 months. Infused oils and tinctures are the best to extract the most antioxidants. If you want pain relief, melt some beeswax into your oil for a salve and a relaxing massage lotion.

Be careful about eucalyptus essential oils (there is a reason I tend not to encourage people to make them). Eucalyptus essential oil is toxic when taken orally. It's also not recommended as a salve or steam inhalation for children under the age of 2.

Our next herb caught my interest because of the history behind it. Aspirin is "only" around 125 years old. So what did people do for pain relief before this? Well, let's meet a member of the humble daisy family!

9

FEVERFEW

Tanacetum Parthenium

Aspirin was "created" in the late 19th century, and it was the salicylic acid from willow bark that led to this discovery. Despite coming from a completely different plant, feverfew was the medieval version of aspirin or the aspirin of the 18th century.

Feverfew is a member of the daisy family, and there is a striking resemblance. You will also hear it referred to as a bachelor's button, wild chamomile, or feather few. Like dandelions, feverfew is highly underrated.

THE PLANT'S NAME GIVES AWAY SOME OF THE BENEFITS

Feverfew has traditionally been used for fever and migraines. It has also been a popular choice for other pain relief, such as stomach aches, toothaches, period pain, and rheumatoid arthritis. European folk medicine used it for allergies, psoriasis, asthma, dizziness, and nausea.

The active compounds in feverfew are flavonoids and over 30 sesquiterpene lactones, chemical compounds that are essential for health and a potential treatment for cancer and cardiovascular disease. The plant has anti-inflammatory properties and may also help as a mild sedative.

THE PERENNIAL THAT KEEPS ON GIVING

Imagine flowers that look like daisies on leaves resembling parsley with a lovely strong scent. It grows annually in cooler climates, but if you live somewhere a little warmer, it may return as a perennial. Either way, we have five steps to make sure you have plenty.

Step 1: Scatter Your Seeds

Plant feverfew seeds indoors 5 to 7 weeks before the last frost for an early start. Once the last frost has passed, you can direct sow by lightly scattering the seeds and covering them with a generous sprinkling of soil so that light can get to them. Spray with a mister to keep the soil moist. If you are growing indoors, leave them near a window with plenty of light. Germination takes around 10 to 14 days.

Step 2: Ensuring Healthy Feverfew

You can transplant feverfew seedlings once there are at least two true leaves, and the last frost has passed. Give the plants a good watering after transplanting. Feverfew likes full sun, but for hotter zones, provide some shade too. Usually, you only need to water feverfew twice a week if there is no rain.

Step 3: Do You Need to Take Cuttings?

Feverfew self-seeds, so you will likely see new plants popping up next spring. You can take a 4 to 5-inch cutting in summer and replant it in fresh soil. It might be best to leave the container on a heat mat to help the new roots develop. It's also possible to divide the roots. Dig up a mature feverfew plant; a large taproot and many rhizomes will branch off. Cut the root ball into 3 or 4 pieces and replant them 18 inches apart—deadhead flowers to promote the growth of more flowers and prevent rapid spreading.

Step 4: How to Harvest Feverfew

Up to 85 percent of the sesquiterpene lactones are found in the leaves (Pareek et al., 2011), so the leaves are more frequently used for medicinal purposes. Nevertheless, all of the aerial parts of feverfew are edible. You can harvest the leaves at any time of the growing season by pinching them off.

The flowers are best harvested as they start to bloom because this is when they have the highest levels of essential oils. Aim to harvest flowers mid-morning once the dew has dried. You can cut entire stems but don't harvest more than a third of a plant.

Step 5: Preparing Feverfew for Storage

If you aren't planning to use your harvest fresh, bundle 4 or 5 stems together and hang them upside down in a dry, shaded area. It takes about one week for all the parts to dry. You might wonder why I always say to hang bundles upside down. This way, all the essential oils flow to the leaves and flowers, increasing the health benefits. After drying, separate the leaves and flowers from the stem and store them in an airtight container in a dark place.

HOW TO USE FEVERFEW SAFELY

Fresh leaves and flowers can be used to make herbal teas and tinctures. That being said, if you have extra dried parts, they can also be used. For teas, 2 or 3 leaves are an excellent medicinal amount, but you may need a bit of honey as the leaves are quite bitter. Some people will chew on fresh leaves for pain in the gums, but if you notice any pain in your mouth, stop. The leaves and flowers can be made into a poultice or a compress to help sore muscles.

Feverfew isn't recommended for children under two years old or pregnant women (it could cause early contractions and miscarriage). There isn't enough research on feverfew and breastfeeding women, so check with your doctor first. Feverfew may slow blood clotting, and if you are taking medications processed by the liver, speak to your doctor in case of interactions.

Because feverfew is so similar to other daisy family members, this chart below will help you identify the right plant.

	Flower	Stem	Leaves
Feverfew	½ to 1 inch in diameter with 10 to 30 short white petals. There are three small teeth on the tips. The yellow center is button-shaped.	Grows upright and smooth without any hairs at the base of the stem and more hairs towards the flower	1 ½ to 4 inches long and up to 2 ½ inches wide. They are in opposite pairs with a slightly citrus odor when crushed in the fingers.
Daisy	Flowers can be 1 to 2 inches across (more for some varieties). The petals grow outward and in multiple layers.	Typically grows 24 to 36 inches tall with a thick stem.	Leaves are oblong with jagged edges and a pointy tip. There are fewer leaves, and they are mainly around the base.
Chamomile	The diameter of the flower is often between 3 and 4 inches. Petals tend to point slightly down, with a single row of petals.	It can grow to be from 6 inches up to 3 feet. The stems look more spindly.	The leaves are thinner and grow sporadically along the stem.

In the next chapter, we are heading to Asia for a traditional spice that has long been used to balance our energy.

10

GINSENG

Ginseng - American: Panax Quinquefolius
Ginseng - Chinese: Panax Ginseng

Ginseng is a distinctive root - if you squint your eyes a little, you can almost see the outline of a human body. This is why it has been seen as a cure-all spice. In Traditional Chinese Medicine, ginseng is used more as a preventative measure. The spice is used to restore qi, our vital energy. When qi is imbalanced, we are more susceptible to diseases.

There are two main types of ginseng: American and Asian. We will cover both.

AMERICAN GINSENG VS. ASIAN GINSENG

American and Asian ginseng have high levels of antioxidants, ginsenosides, and gintonin, which help fight oxidative stress and inflammation. Regular use of ginseng can improve cognitive function, and studies have shown that ginseng regulates hormonal changes due to stress, easing symptoms of stress-related anxiety and depression (Lee & Rhee, 2017).

With anti-bacterial, anti-fungal, and anti-viral properties, there is a good chance that both types of ginseng can boost the immune system. The ginsenosides may help prevent abnormal cell growth that can lead to cancer while also helping to control blood sugar levels, especially red ginseng (which has been left to mature for more than six years).

The main difference comes with the concentration of the active ingredients. American ginseng is thought to be better used as a calming and relaxation remedy and Asian ginseng can give you more of an energy boost.

HOW TO GROW AND CARE FOR GINSENG

When it comes to growing these types of ginseng, their needs are similar, but the choice between them may depend on your climate. Generally, Asian ginseng thrives in hardiness zones 5 to 9, while American ginseng is better suited for zones 3 to 7.

Step 1: A Plant to Start in the Fall

Ginseng seeds need a cold period, so plant the seeds directly outside in the fall, possibly early winter, before any signs of frost. Ideally, you want to try and create a woodland environment for ginseng, and it will thrive in partial to full shade in an area with good air circulation.

Leave seeds to soak in a solution of 90 percent water and 10 percent bleach for 10 minutes to prevent fungi from growing. Then plant the seeds about ½ an inch into the soil with 2 to 3 inches between each seed. Cover the seeds with a 2-inch layer of leaves and straw (mulch) to protect them over the winter.

Step 2: What Does Ginseng Require

Seedlings will appear in the spring but don't panic because it could happen in the summer. It's essential to make sure that, during this growth stage, the plant is watered regularly so that the soil doesn't dry out. It's better to water a little and often. When the plant reaches maturity after at least 3 years, you may only need to water it during drought.

Step 3: Roots for New Plants

Digging up your ginseng and replanting some of the roots is an excellent idea. This is because the plant will grow faster from the root than a seed, and you will have a larger harvest sooner. They have to be at least two years old before you replant a root to grow a new plant.

Another great idea to keep growing more ginseng is to harvest a plant with ripe berries. Squeeze the berry between your fingers and pop it into the space where you harvested the plant. If you feel there is a better location in your garden, you can also replant it elsewhere.

Step 4: Techniques to Harvest Ginseng

Between years 4 and 6, you can start harvesting your ginseng. At this point, ginseng is white, and there will be at least four leaves that will begin to turn yellow. For more mature red ginseng, it can take up to 8 years. But don't worry, you can harvest some and leave others to mature.

Carefully move the soil around the base of the plant. You might want to use a hand trowel or soil knife. The key is to try not to damage the roots. Remove enough soil to see the larger taproots. Then dig it up.

Step 5: How to Store Your Fresh Ginseng

Once washed and dried, fresh ginseng can last in the fridge for a few weeks. Drying ginseng shouldn't be rushed because you risk losing some of the health benefits. To air-dry them, they need temperatures of around 70°F for one week or two. During this time, check for mold, as this could be a sign that the temperature isn't right or there is too much humidity. The roots will start to shrink and will snap when completely dry. The roots can be stored whole or ground into a powder. As long as it has been dried correctly, ginseng can last for up to 5 years.

HERBAL REMEDIES AND CULINARY USES

A tincture is a simple way to take ginseng daily, as are teas, and you can use fresh or dried roots. Try adding dried ginseng to whole coffee beans or powder to coffee and smoothies for some variations. Ginseng iced tea is refreshing with a slice of lemon. Ginseng can also be made into a salve to help balance the skin.

As ginseng isn't recommended as a daily supplement for more than a couple of months, it is safest to find ways to add it to your cooking for regular use—the spice pairs particularly well with chicken, pork, and beef and especially in soups and stir-fries. You can also experiment with ginseng, citrus fruits, cinnamon, and ginger.

American ginseng has an incredible lifespan, even outliving humans, but fortunately, I can't testify to this. However, considering a well-cared-for ginseng plant can live for up to 15 years plus up to 5 years of storage, waiting those first years proves very worthwhile.

The next chapter will look at a plant native to North America, found in rich shady soils with bright raspberry-like fruit: goldenseal!

11

GOLDENSEAL

Hydrastis Canadensis

Goldenseal is native to North America, and despite little evidence of its health benefits, it is still a prevalent herb in the US. Aside from the potential health benefits, it's an excellent idea to have native plants in your garden.

Native plants are easier to grow because the conditions are perfect for their needs. They are crucial for the ecosystem, providing beneficial insects and animals shelter. They also require less maintenance, water, and nutrients, making life easier. As goldenseal is at high risk of extinction because of over-cultivation, we could all do our part and grow this herbal plant.

WHAT IS GOLDENSEAL?

Goldenseal is a member of the buttercup family and a perennial herb. Sometimes, this plant is called yellow root because of the color of the roots. It produces bright red to burgundy berries, but it's not the berries that are prized for medicinal benefits; it's the roots.

Native Americans used goldenseal for itchy eyes, mouth ulcers, and tuberculosis. Today, it is still a common ingredient in herbal eyewashes for allergies and infections. The berberine in goldenseal has been shown to have antimicrobial properties. For this, it is often used to treat infections and cuts. It may also ease stomach aches, sore throat, symptoms of colds, congestion, and respiratory problems.

HAVING A LITTLE PATIENCE WITH GOLDENSEAL

Because the rhizomes are used, there are many similarities between growing ginseng and goldenseal.

Step 1: Getting the Location Right for Goldenseal

Start seeds in the fall. It's often best to plant them directly in the outdoor soil. Plant seeds at a depth of ½ to ¾ inches and cover with a good 2-inch layer of mulch.

The area should be well-drained, so if you have a slope in your garden, you can take advantage of this space. The plant prefers partial shade, and signs of life should appear in the spring.

Step 2: Low-Maintenance Homesteading

You won't need to do a lot for healthy growth. Keep an eye on the soil moisture so that it doesn't dry out, but rainwater should suffice unless there are times of drought. You do need to make sure that no weeds pop up. Mulch should help with this, and you can pick the odd ones that may appear.

Step 3: How to Propagate Goldenseal for Rhizomes

Within 5 to 7 years, the rhizomes will have matured enough to take cuttings for a new plant. This is sensible because maturity takes 3 to 5 years to grow from a root. You must cut a piece of the rhizome between ½ an inch and 1 inch, and the cutting should have thin fibrous roots and at least one bud. Plant the cutting 1 ½ to 2 inches into the ground, ensuring the bud faces upward.

Step 4: Harvesting Your Rhizomes

The ideal time to harvest goldenseal is in September or October. The medicinal benefits are transferred to the roots as the leaves fade and die back before the plant goes dormant. Harvesting at this time also gives the plant a chance to self-seed. Like ginseng, carefully dig around the plant base to expose the rhizome and fibrous roots before removing the plant.

Be sure to wash the rhizomes immediately to reduce the bacteria risk. Soak them in a bucket of water, but you should make sure to get the dirt out of any nooks and crannies.

Step 5: Preserving Cleaned Goldenseal

Again, you can keep fresh goldenseal in the fridge for one week or two, but drying is best for long-term storage. Drying typically requires temperatures of between 85°F and 95°F, higher if your climate is humid. The outer parts turn darker, but the inside should remain yellow. After 5 to 10 days, snap a piece to ensure it is completely dry.

HOW TO USE GOLDENSEAL

The berries can't be eaten, but the leaves can. You can pick leaves as and when you want them to make teas. The leaves don't have the same concentration of active ingredients, but they are also less bitter. Fresh or dried roots can also be used to make tea.

Instead of just making a tincture and taking a few drops, try adding some of your tincture to water and other drinks for something different. For topical use, infuse oil or take it a step further with a salve. Use the leaves for a decoction and a poultice.

Generally speaking, goldenseal is considered safe for most people, but I wouldn't advise it for children, pregnant or breastfeeding women, or anyone with health conditions and/or taking medication because of the lack of studies. If you notice any allergic reaction, stop taking it straight away.

If you have read my first book *The Homesteader Herbal Handbook,* you will know how much of a fan I am of parsley. Following the same theme, the next chapter will examine a relative of one of my favorite culinary herbs.

12

GOTU KOLA

Centella Asiatica

Gotu kola is a popular perennial herb within Ayurvedic medicine and Traditional Chinese Medicine because of the wide range of potential benefits, many now backed by science. These lovely small fan-shaped leaves have no taste or smell, so they are perfect for those who want to add greens to their diet but aren't keen on veggie flavors.

WHAT MAKES GOTU KOLA SPECIAL?

Starting with the brain, gotu kola may help improve memory and cognitive function. The potential is so exciting that it could even be used to treat Alzheimer's, with studies on mice showing improved memory and nerve function as well as a positive impact on behavioral abnormalities (Soumyanath et al., 2012). It can also improve sleep and lower symptoms of anxiety and depression.

Other possible benefits include improved circulation, reduced inflammation and pain, and a detox effect on the body. For topical use, gotu kola could minimize the appearance of stretch marks and heal various types of wounds. It is more frequently used today in the US and Europe for varicose veins, psoriasis, and minor wounds. Finally, the asiatic acid and the antioxidants in gotu kola may help to reduce the risk of different diseases, including certain cancers.

GETTING THE RIGHT GROWING CONDITIONS FOR GOTU KOLA

If the conditions are just right, such as warm wetlands, gotu kola can be invasive. It grows well in hardiness zones 9 to 11. For those in lower hardiness zones, you will need a greenhouse, or you can grow it as an indoor herb. Remember, this is a creeping plant, and left to its own devices, it can spread up to 3 feet wide.

Step 1: The One Mistake Never to Make

Some will say that gotu kola is notoriously tricky to grow, but there is an excellent chance of germination as long as your seeds never dry out. You can start the seeds indoors in late fall or wait until all signs of frost have passed to sow them directly outdoors.

I prefer biodegradable starting pots so there is less root disturbance later on. Pop one seed in each container, gently pushing it into moist soil. Keep a distance between the seeds of about 9 to 12 inches if sowing in your soil. Depending on your temperatures, seeds should germinate between days 30 and 90. If you have a heat mat, this can encourage germination—remember to keep an eye on the soil moisture.

Step 2: Transplanting and Caring for Gotu Kola

When you have spotted those true leaves coming through, it's time to transplant the seedlings. Many people choose to grow gotu kola in containers for the first year because it's easier to manage in colder temperatures. Gotu kola loves rich soil, so when you transplant the seedlings, add plenty of compost to your fresh soil, and don't forget to ensure the new soil is thoroughly watered. Leave the container in partial shade. For the winter months, move the container indoors.

Step 3: Divide and Conquer

Each stem you see touching the soil will have roots. Once the plant has had time to mature, typically the following season, you can separate the rooted runners (those growing around the edges) from the main plant by snipping the roots with scissors. Gently lift the separated plant and place it in a new home.

Step 4: Super Simple Harvesting

There are two harvesting options. First, when you dig up a plant to divide the roots, you can take this opportunity to harvest a large yield by replanting half the plant and then harvesting all the leaves and stems of the rest. This might be helpful if the roots are creeping to the point of overcrowding in your garden. Alternatively, harvest the stems at the base when you need the leaves.

Step 5: Watch Out When Storing Gotu Kola in the Fridge

The fresh leaves you harvest are temperature sensitive. If the leaves turn black in the fridge, it's because it's too cold for them. When the temperature is right, the stems can be cut shorter and placed in a glass of water. Then keep the glass in a plastic bag for up to 1 week.

As with many other leaves, you can air-dry them, though this might take longer because of the higher moisture content. Do the "leaf snap trick" to test them. Interestingly, the most effective way to dry gotu kola is by freeze-drying. This involves placing leaves on a tray and leaving them in the freezer for at least one week. Take one leaf out of the freezer and leave it to thaw. If it returns to its original color, all the moisture has dried out during the freezing process. If not, leave them for a few more days and repeat the test.

Honestly, I have never tried freeze-drying, but it's on my to-do list. I would love to hear your results with this method.

HOW TO ADD GOTU KOLA TO YOUR DIET AND WHO SHOULDN'T

Harvest young leaves to add a little heat to salads and sandwiches. Cooked, they are excellent in curries, stir-fries, and soups and pair well with fish and vegetables. For skin healing, you can make a poultice or an infused oil. If you grind your dried leaves into a powder and mix with water until you get a paste, you have another topical use.

Use your infused oil for a head massage for a little bit of luxury. While you have your infused oil out, add some baking soda to make a face mask. With regular use, you may notice fewer wrinkles and firmer skin!

For those taking medications that impact the liver, medicines for diabetes, cholesterol-lowering drugs, sedatives, and diuretics, please speak to your doctor in case of any interactions. Also, gotu kola should only be used for up to 6 weeks. Then, take a 2-week break before taking your herbal remedy again.

I add dried crushed leaves to my scented candles. Yes, I know this doesn't add to the smell, but it still means I can inhale some of the benefits. In fact, I even add the petals of the next flower to the same candles for a further boost of health and some scent.

Speaking of flowers, you might recognize hibiscus as a popular splash of color in most gardens, but there are more reasons to grow this little delight!

13

HIBISCUS

Hibiscus Rosa-Sinensis

Hibiscus flowers are beautiful, growing to around 4 to 6 inches, and have a lovely range of colors, including orange, yellow, red, pink, and even multicolored. If you are lucky, you can grow flowers with a rich main color and a contrasting rim. I love these flowers for their appearance and health benefits.

HOW CAN DIFFERENT PARTS OF THE HIBISCUS PLANT HEAL?

The hibiscus is an excellent homesteading plant because we can use all parts of the plants for healing, so there is very little waste. As you can imagine, different plant parts will have different concentrations of active compounds, so they will treat different ailments. The roots are used to help with the symptoms of coughs, colds, and infectious diseases. The leaves are better as an anti-inflammatory and may also work as a gentle laxative if you have digestive issues.

Hibiscus flowers have a high level of antioxidants, including vitamin C, as well as other crucial vitamins and minerals. Flowers can support the digestive system too. They may help relieve inflammation of the digestive tract, protect it, and kill bacteria in the intestines. People have also used hibiscus flowers to lower fever. Hibiscus tea might help lower blood pressure and, possibly for some, lower cholesterol too.

5 STEPS TO A HEALTHY HIBISCUS PLANT AND YIELD

Hibiscus can be a little fussier than other flowers in terms of temperature. It grows best in tropical and subtropical climates and will likely flower for most of the year. In other climates, it can be grown as an annual.

Step 1: Choose a Snug Container

There is no reason you can't plant hibiscus seeds directly in the garden, but I have found that mine do better in containers. The roots are happier with a slightly tighter fit, so despite the large size of the flower, don't feel you need a huge container. Containers also give you a chance to grow this as an indoor plant. Wait until spring to plant the seeds so you can take advantage of the full sun.

To speed up germination, soak the hibiscus seeds in water overnight. Plant them in a container with holes in the bottom for good drainage. Pop the seeds around ½ inch into the soil. With temperatures of 75°F to 85°F, seedlings should appear within 2 to 3 weeks. The stems of seedlings are very delicate, so make sure they are protected from the wind.

Step 2: Hibiscus—The Fussy Drinker

If you need to transplant the seedlings, dig a hole big enough for the root ball to fit. Once in, start filling the hole with soil but stop halfway to give the soil a good soaking, then top up the rest of the hole. If transplanting to your garden, keep the seedlings 2 to 3 feet apart for sufficient space. You might want to add a layer of mulch to help with water retention.

When it comes to watering, please don't give them cold water because it will shock them. Ideally, the water should be around room temperature. For hibiscus grown in containers, water every day, and for hibiscus grown outdoors, water every other day. But beware, yellow leaves are a sign of overwatering.

Deadhead the flowers before they seed so that energy is redirected to growing more flowers. If you are able to grow hibiscus as a perennial, you should give it a light prune in the spring, removing no more than a third of the stems. This will help reduce the risk of hibiscus-loving bugs.

Step 3: Replicating Your Hibiscus

Choose a cutting that has lots of smooth leaves. Cut the stem at an angle to improve water absorption and trim away the lower leaves. You can either place the cutting in a glass of water or straight into fresh soil that is kept very moist. In both cases, keep the cutting out of direct sunlight. In water, the roots will have formed enough to plant in the soil after about four weeks. In soil, it will take eight weeks.

Step 4: Harvesting the Various Plant Parts

Around 7 to 10 days after the flowers have bloomed, the outer part of the flower, the calyx, becomes fleshy. You can cut these off with a pair of clippers. The best blooms are in spring and fall, not necessarily because of the temperature but because this plant actually likes shorter days.

To harvest the leaves, you can trim them off as and when you need them or take advantage of pruning for a larger harvest. If your hibiscus is an annual, harvest all the leaves before any frost appears so they don't go to waste.

Step 5: Storing These Beautiful Flowers

Those parts you don't want to use fresh should be dried for long-term use. We use the same drying techniques we have seen for the leaves and roots. Place the parts on a tray or rack and leave them in a well-ventilated area for 1 to 2 weeks until they snap.

To dry the flowers, stick your finger inside to remove the pea-sized seed. You can save these for next year! Then spread the flowers on a rack and leave them for 3 to 5 days. They can be left whole or crumbled slightly.

USING THE VARIOUS PLANT PARTS

Hibiscus leaves are particularly good for the hair and skin, so you could try infusing them in coconut oil for topical use. Some people love the leaves in tea, but they have quite a robust and tangy flavor. All of the parts can be used fresh or dry to make tea. Most people prefer to use the flowers for herbal remedies.

Aside from a tincture, a lovely way for all the family to benefit from hibiscus flowers is in syrup, especially for coughs, colds, and sore throats. If you are going to make a tincture, add the roots too. The flowers are also fantastic for skin treatments. Try turning dried flowers into a powder, and mix with baking powder and rose water for a face mask.

My hibiscus needed an extra boost for growing, as it wasn't getting enough nutrients from the soil. Instead of using fertilizer and risking those nasty chemicals in our systems, I used kitchen scraps to make compost and mixed some leaves to use as mulch.

You may have heard of the city that was so good it was named twice. Well, in the next chapter, we will discover the plant that was so good they named it twice!

14

KAVA KAVA

Piper Methysticum

Honestly, I have no idea why it's called kava kava; in fact, many people just call it kava. I do know that it has many mental health benefits. Traditionally, kava was used in the Pacific Islands as a ceremonial drink. People would either chew the roots or crush or grind them before adding them to water. This drink was supposed to improve their communication with the higher spirits. Studies today focus on anxiety.

THE STUDIES ON KAVA

It was only about a decade ago that Australians carried out a ground-breaking clinical trial on the effectiveness of kava on anxiety. The 8-week study saw 75 people with generalized anxiety disorder (GAD) given either kava or a placebo. Not only did the results show reduced anxiety in the group taking kava, but 26 percent of those in the group were also in remission from their symptoms by the end of the trial (University of Melbourne, 2013).

Though most of the research on kava focused on anxiety, the kavalactones in the roots may also protect neurons from damage and reduce lower back pain. Because of its ability to reduce anxiety and stress, kava might be a more natural way of reducing stress-induced insomnia.

4 STEPS TO GROWING YOUR OWN MOOD ENHANCER

No, that's not a typo—there are only four steps to growing kava. A bizarre fact is that all kava seeds are sterile, and the only way to grow kava is by cutting. And to do this, you will have to either know someone with a healthy kava plant or start by purchasing one.

Step 1: Propagating Kava

Kava is a perennial shrub and fairly robust. That being said, propagating new plants is still a sensible idea.

Outdoors and hardiness zones 11 and 12, plants can grow 10 to 15 feet tall. For other zones and smaller shrubs, kava can be grown in containers and overwintered indoors.

Before propagating a new plant, the mother plant should be at least two years old with a minimum height of 12 inches. For greater success, it's essential to choose the right stem. There should be 2 to 5 nodes on a stem that is at least ½ an inch in diameter.

Rather than planting your cutting vertically, it must be placed horizontally in the soil. The eye (the node's large circle) must be facing upward. Cover with enough soil to make sure no parts are visible. The soil needs to be kept moist, and you may want to cover the container for the first few weeks to improve humidity levels. New shoots should appear in a few weeks.

Step 2: Make Sure Not to Kill Your Plant

Be sure your young kava plants have shade and are not exposed to direct sunlight. The soil should constantly be moist but not soaking. Once the seedlings reach 12 inches, it's time to transplant them. Water the hole before you add the young plant to the new container to help the roots develop. In the first 1 to 3 months, most of the energy is focused on root growth, so don't worry if you don't see too much happening above the soil. Take care of weeds because they can take over and kill your plant!

Step 3: When to Harvest Kava Roots

The amounts of kavalactones increase as kava matures. In its native conditions and with enough time, roots can grow up to 2 feet in diameter and 6 feet long! Once kava reaches 3 to 5 years old and around 6 feet in height, it's a good time to harvest the roots.

Cut back the stems of the plant to the first node. This will make it easier to work with. Dig around the soil to loosen it up, carefully moving away as much as possible to expose the root without causing any damage. Once enough soil has been removed, you can pull up the roots. If you have grown kava in a container, turning it upside down and brushing off the soil might be easier. Cut the root into smaller pieces, throwing away any that are damaged or showing signs of mold. When washed and dried, healthy roots have a lovely shine.

Step 4: How to Keep Kava Roots

Kava roots have a very high water content, as much as 80 percent. The roots are also hygroscopic, meaning they attract and absorb moisture from the air. For this reason, air-drying can be very difficult. You can cut the roots into slices, place them on a baking tray and dry them in the oven at 140°F until they are fully dried. Storing the dried kava in a moisture-resistant container is really important. If kava gets damp, you can dry it again, but it will lose some health benefits each time you do.

USING KAVA THE SENSIBLE WAY

If you want to prepare kava traditionally, grind the dried roots into a powder and put the powder into a straining bag. Place it in a bowl of warm water and gently knead the bag. You will notice the water turning brown. Don't worry if it feels a bit oily; this is the kavalactones being released. After 10 minutes, you have a traditional kava drink. Avoid using hot water to make drinks because anything over 140°F can kill the active ingredients, plus give the drink an overbearing taste. Fresh roots are perfect for tinctures.

Kava has a similar effect on the brain as alcohol, slowing down the messages from the brain to the body. For this reason, care should be taken. In the first place, only use the roots. The leaves and stems are poisonous and can cause liver damage. I would only recommend drinking or taking kava at night. This way, if it does cause drowsiness, you aren't at risk of having an accident. Don't use kava with alcohol or sedatives, and take care if you are on other medications or have liver problems.

In the next chapter, we will take a closer look at a plant with a name to suit its elegant leaves, the lady fern.

15

LADY FERNS

Athyrium Filix-Femina

Normally, I don't bother much with scientific names, but this one catches my attention. The scientific name for lady ferns is Athyrium filix-femina. Athyrium comes from the Greek word athyros meaning doorless. This is because lady ferns don't flower. Instead, they release spores from the underside of their leaves. These spores are slow-opening and unhinged. Filix-femina means fern woman in Greek.

THE SURPRISING BENEFITS OF LADY FERNS

There hasn't been extensive research on lady ferns, but they have been used in traditional medicines, and their health benefits are still well-known today. One of the most popular uses is for pain relief, for headaches, sore muscles and joints, and even for labor pain. It may also help with indigestion and possibly kill parasitic worms, though this has to be a strong decoction.

For coughs and colds, lady ferns can provide pretty fast relief and help open the air passages for those with asthma and bronchitis. With antiseptic and antimicrobial properties, this plant may also help cure sores.

One word of warning, if you have a dog, try to keep them away from lady ferns. It's unlikely they will ingest a lot, but it can be toxic to dogs!

GIVING THE LADY ALL SHE NEEDS

Lady ferns are native to Canada and most of North America, making them a great choice for everyone as long as they have slightly acidic and moist soil. As they don't produce flowers, it's another plant that we can't sow the seeds.

Step 1: Finding Your Spores

There are two ways to source your spores. The easiest is to buy them or join an international fern society that offers spore exchanges. If you are going to collect your own spores, be sure to have permission from the landowner first. You might need a magnifying glass too.

On the underside of the leaves, there is a sporangium, a case with the spores inside a thin wall. The best time to collect spores is when the casing starts to break down. The spores also plump up and change color, most likely deep browns and burgundies. Cut a leaf and place the leaf in an envelope. The spores should fall off within 24 hours. Keep them in a cool place until spring.

When spring comes, sprinkle the spores onto fresh, moist soil. They don't need to be covered with soil. Place the container in a clear plastic bag and leave it in a warm area but not in direct sunlight.

Step 2: From Spores to Ferns

After a few weeks, shoots should appear, and they will look like little heart leaves. During this growth period, you only need to keep the soil moist, as you would find in shaded woodlands. You will start to see the baby fern leaves sprouting from the heart leaves.

By fall, they will be ready to transplant to their final home, somewhere with partial shade and well-drained soil. The soil should never dry out. If you notice the leaves starting to grow brown or wilt, it means they need water. If you aren't growing lady ferns in your garden, you will want to repot them in larger containers every 2 to 3 years.

Step 3: Propagating Lady Ferns

Spring is also the best time to propagate lady ferns. The easiest way is to separate the plant through root division. Remove the plant from the container and brush away the soil. Choose a section of rhizome that has a good amount of foliage. You may be able to break the roots with your hands or with a sharp knife—place them in a clean container with fresh soil and some compost.

Step 4: Harvesting This Ornamental Plant

There are three parts of the plant we can harvest, and I try to make the most of propagating, replanting, and harvesting simultaneously. With a mature plant, I can separate it three ways, one mother plant, one new plant, and one for harvesting the roots and leaves. You can also harvest leaves when needed.

In the spring, lady ferns produce edible fiddleheads at the base of the plant. You can harvest these (before they reach 4 inches) and use these for cooking.

Step 5: In Case You Need to Store Lady Fern

Fresh lady fern leaves will stay fresh in the fridge for around three weeks in water or between damp paper towels. You can put the leaves flat on a tray and leave them for about two weeks to dry, and some people put them between two sheets of paper and then between books to use for crafts! Rhizomes can be sliced and dried in the same way.

Fiddleheads can be stored in an airtight container or in water in the fridge. If you add them to water, you must change the water daily. To freeze fiddleheads, boil them for a couple of minutes first.

MAKING HERBAL REMEDIES WITH LADY FERN

Lady fern roots and leaves are best for teas, decoctions, and tinctures. If you have dried your harvest, you can use the parts whole or powdered. Use your fiddleheads as you would other green vegetables and cook them by steaming or boiling them and then sautéing in oil or butter. Your fiddleheads can be canned for long-term preservation.

If you want to entertain the crowd, lady fern fiddleheads are an impressive substitute for other, more common greens. It's interesting to hear how people describe the flavor, too, because it's difficult to pinpoint the exact taste.

Lady fern is another plant that doesn't exactly see fast results and is generally not grown for its taste. However, the next herb is versatile in the kitchen and is ready to harvest sooner than later.

16

LEMON BALM

Melissa Officinalis

I love lemon balm because it confuses my senses. As a member of the mint family, there is a rich scent of mint, but as the name suggests, there is also a lovely citrus kick. Back in the middle ages, lemon balm leaves were steeped in wine to lift the spirits, and I must admit, it's a good way to improve the health benefits of a glass of wine.

WHAT MAKES LEMON BALM PERFECT FOR HERBALISM?

There are more than 100 phytochemicals in lemon balm. Some of the most significant are citronellal, geraniol (giving it a slight rose smell), linalool (a lavender scent), and various flavonoids. The high level of antioxidants has led lemon balm to be investigated for the treatment of Alzheimer's and dementia. One study showed that lemon balm extract decreased lung cancer cell growth (Andújar, 2020).

Lemon balm has antidepressant, antispasmodic, antihistaminic, and antiviral properties. This fantastic little plant can help with sleep problems, stress, and anxiety and improve mood. It may help to reduce headaches and treat wounds. For me, it's a great allrounder that is often underestimated.

FROM SEED TO STORAGE

It's a perennial plant that thrives in US hardiness zones 4 to 9. It can handle temperatures as low as -20°F, but it may struggle in hot temperatures. The plant can grow up to 24 inches wide and the same in height with oval leaves and clusters of white flowers in the summer, a particular favorite of honeybees.

Step 1: Find the Right Location

Lemon balm likes a decent amount of sunlight, around 6 to 8 hours, but it doesn't mind a bit of shade. It's also not fussy about the soil it grows in. However, it will do better with soil with a slightly higher pH level.

Seeds can be planted indoors eight weeks before the last frost or planted outside once the frost has passed. The seeds need light to germinate, so only plant them ¼ of an inch into the soil outdoors and just add a sprinkle of soil if you are planting them indoors. Use a mister to spray the seeds, and within 14 days, they should germinate.

Step 2: Encouraging Healthy Growth

The most challenging thing about growing lemon balm is keeping it under control. Like mint, it tends to spread, although not as badly. It can spread via the roots underground, and it will also self-seed, and new plants will pop up. For this reason, many prefer to keep lemon balm in containers, and deadheading will help control the growth of new plants.

Lemon balm needs frequent watering while it establishes, but it is fairly drought-resistant once mature. Prune your plant to keep it healthy, but you only need to cut back any dead or damaged stems. In the winter, cut the whole plant back to around 2 inches from the base. It sounds drastic, but it will bounce back in spring.

Step 3: How to Take Lemon Balm Cuttings

The cutting you take will depend on the season. If you want to propagate lemon balm in spring, you need to cut a stem a few inches from the tip of the new growth. In the fall, it should be a stem that hasn't flowered that is cut longer, almost close to the base. Root growth will be helped if you dip the end in honey before planting them in a container. Be sure to water the cutting straight away and keep it out of direct sunlight. After a month, the roots should have developed, and it is safe to transplant into a bigger container.

Step 4: Easy Harvesting of Lemon Balm

During the growing season, you can harvest leaves by pinching off the stems you want to use. The lower, more mature leaves will have the strongest flavor. In summer, the older leaves start to become bitter, so these are best for drying rather than fresh use.

When you prune your lemon balm in spring, you can take a larger harvest but no more than a third of the plant. Naturally, when you cut the plant right back in winter, you will have your biggest harvest.

Step 5: Lemon Balm Preservation

Add lemon balm to a glass of water to stay fresh in the fridge for around two weeks. I really like the ice cube tray trick with water or oil to freeze lemon balm. Either keep the leaves coiled up whole or chop them first. To air-dry lemon balm, it's best to bundle stems and hang them upside down in a paper bag. Punch some holes in the bag for proper air circulation. Leaves tend to fall off the stem when dry, and the bag will catch them. It only takes a couple of days to dry. Dried lemon balm lasts for about a year.

EASY HERBAL REMEDIES WITH LEMON BALM

Teas and tinctures are ideal. In fact, in the study on cancer cells, the best results were those where alcohol was used for extraction. I like olive oil to infuse lemon balm to make hair and skin products.

Lemon balm goes well with most fruits, so add lemon balm leaves to your jam recipes. You can include it in your soups and sauces as well as in baked goods like cookies. I think the best thing is to explore using lemon balm as a culinary herb. It can pair well with so many flavors, from pestos to ginger!

In the next chapter, we will explore another popular flower that is also underrated for its health benefits and the food it provides for beneficial insects.

17

MARIGOLD

Calendula Officinalis

Fun fact about marigolds, they are also sometimes used as a natural colorant in food. Farmers sometimes add petals to chicken feed to make their egg yolks darker, and when added to butter, there is a deeper shade of orange. There are different types of marigolds, but the Calendula marigold is said to have the most benefits.

MARIGOLDS—MORE THAN PRETTY PETALS

Some of the active compounds in marigolds are calendulin, calendric acid, carotenoids, and flavonoids. Extracts can have a powerful effect on oxidative stress and damage to cells, especially when it comes to eye health. It can help with conjunctivitis and eye inflammation, as well as helping to prevent age-related damage to the eyes.

With antibacterial, antiviral, antifungal, and immune-boosting properties, this magical little flower can help with a wide range of skin problems, from diaper rash, varicose veins, and insect bites to cuts, ingrown hairs, and bruises. It may also aid in digestion and reduce muscle cramps and spasms.

5 STEPS TO BRIGHTEN YOUR GARDEN AND PANTRY

These annual flowers are most commonly found in orange, white, yellow, red, and sometimes multicolored. The nice thing about them is that if you deadhead them, they produce striking blooms throughout summer and into fall.

Step 1: A Little Soil Preparation

They aren't fussy about the soil type but they do thrive in fertile soil. It's a good idea to dig up around 6 inches of soil and mix in some compost to start. Marigolds need sun. If left in a cool, shaded area, they are at risk of powdery mildew. Sow the seeds once the last frost has passed, and even better, wait a couple of weeks for the soil to warm up. There is little benefit to starting seeds indoors because they do so well outside; in containers, they may become cramped.

Plant seeds around 1 inch into the soil and at least 1 inch apart. It usually only takes about one week for the seeds to sprout. Soon after, you should thin them out to around 10 inches apart.

Step 2: How to Care for Calendula Marigolds

The only thing marigolds really need is water. Watch for the top layer of soil to almost dry out, and then water well. Always water marigolds at the base and avoid getting the leaves wet because of powdery mildew.

Don't be tempted to fertilize marigolds; you will have lots of luscious leaves but not the brightest blooms. It's best to add mulch to give the plants the nutrients they need and to help suppress weeds. When the flowers start to dry, pinch them off at the first set of leaves.

Step 3: Growing New Young Plants

Honestly, because it's so easy to grow marigolds from seeds that are annuals, you probably won't find the need to propagate them, but that's not to say it isn't possible. If fewer seeds germinate than you wanted, you can take a cutting.

Choose a stem with at least three leaves but no flowers. Cut the stem between 2 and 6 inches long and remove all leaves except the top set. Pop the stem into fresh soil and leave it in a bright, warm location but not in direct sunlight. Some people put a plastic bag over the stem but make sure it isn't touching the leaves. It will take a few weeks for the roots to develop and a few more weeks before you can transplant them.

Step 4: Harvesting Your Flowers

Marigolds are undeniably beautiful, which can make it tempting to let them bloom for an extra day or two before harvesting them. However, waiting too long may result in wasted flowers. Harvesting the marigolds when they are in full bloom can actually encourage more flowers to grow, allowing for frequent harvesting every few days. For optimal results, it's recommended to pick the flowers in the morning once the dew has dried. However, if that's not possible, it's still better to harvest them at any time of day rather than not at all. When cutting the flowers, be sure to do so at the set of leaves closest to the base of the flower.

Keep an eye out for the flowers that really catch your attention because these are the best seeds to harvest. Watch for the seeds to turn brown. This is when they are ripe enough to harvest. Keep the flowers in a paper bag. After a few days, shake the bag to release the seeds.

Step 5: Storing Marigolds

I prefer to air-dry marigolds as they don't do well in temperatures over 90°F. Lay the heads face down and turn them every couple of days. If you are drying the flowerheads whole, it's crucial to check that the receptacle (the green bit under the petals) is completely dry. This will take longer than the petals to dry. A good tip is that there is still moisture inside if it feels cold. Alternatively, you can pluck the petals off and dry them separately, which will only take a few days.

THE BEST USES OF CALENDULA MARIGOLDS

You can get really creative with marigolds. The petals have a slightly peppery taste and will brighten up salads and rice dishes. They are also great for cakes, especially when added to decorations. Fresh or dried petals can be used to make tea, tinctures, infused oil, and salves. For skin problems, you can rub fresh petals straight onto your skin.

If ingesting, take care if you are on any sleep or anti-anxiety medications because it may increase drowsiness. You should also check with your doctor if you are taking clonazepam, lorazepam, phenobarbital, or zolpidem. When using topically, always start with a small amount to check for allergic reactions.

Any sign of diaper rash with my grandchildren, the first thing we get out is the marigold salve which I make with dried petals and virgin coconut oil. This salve has made a huge difference with my itchy hands too.

Our next plant isn't quite as beautiful, some may even say it's aggressive, but it's worthy of a place on the list. If you have ever been stung by stinging nettles, you won't believe how healthy the leaves are. There is no need to take my word for it; science is also fascinated with nettles.

18

NETTLE

Urtica Dioica

If you look closely at stinging nettles, it seems like they are covered in tiny hairs, but these hairs are actually hollow and act like needles that pass chemicals to our skin when we touch them. Fortunately, we have already discussed many ideas on preparing a cream to counteract this sting in case of accidental contact. We will get rid of the sting before munching on a nettle leaf!

WHY STINGING NETTLES ARE YOUR FRIENDS

Ancient Egyptians would use stinging nettles to ease the symptoms of arthritis, but more interestingly,

Roman troops would rub nettles on them to stay warm! The scientific name makes sense, Urtica dioica is derived from the Latin word uro, which translates to burn. The plant is packed with nutrients like vitamins A, C, K, and some Bs. It contains all the essential amino acids and calcium, iron, magnesium, phosphorus, potassium, sodium, and flavonoids.

These nutrients help protect the body from free radicals and reduce inflammation and may reduce enlarged prostate glands and lower blood pressure. One study showed that taking stinging nettle extract for three months significantly lowered blood sugar levels compared to a placebo (Kianbakht et al., 2013). Ironically, stinging nettle cream may help skin wounds to heal, even burns.

CHOOSING TO GROW AND CARE FOR NETTLES

If you have ever had stinging nettles pop up in your garden, you know how fast they can grow and why many consider them to be weeds. For this reason, it's one of the plants I prefer to grow in a container.

Step 1: Starting Your Seeds

Start nettle seeds the same way we sew most of our culinary herbs. If you want to start them indoors, plan for six weeks before the last frost or sow them into a container when the last frost has passed. Sprinkle the tiny seeds over fresh soil and then sprinkle a thin layer of soil on top. Keep the soil moist by spraying. Germination takes around 14 days.

Step 2: Why You Don't Want Flowers

Caring for nettles is very simple. They like full sun but will tolerate some shade and moist soil while young. Once nettles have matured, you only need to water them if you have had no rain for one week or two. It's a hardy biennial, and at the end of the first season, just cut back any unhealthy stems. In the second year, flowers will grow. Because of the tendency to spread, it's best to deadhead the flowers as soon as possible.

Step 3: The Need for More Nettles

Some people like to leave a few flowers for the pollinators and the chance for seeds to mature. The seeds can be harvested and stored for the following spring. To propagate a new plant from the mother plant, take a cutting from a stem with at least three sets of leaves, trim back the bottom leaves, and place it in a glass of water. Change the water every couple of days, and within a few weeks, the roots will have developed.

Step 4: Handling With Care

Again, for harvesting, you will need gloves. For the best flavor, try to harvest stems before the plant goes to flower because they often go a bit stringy after this. Cut the stem about a third back from the top above a node. The roots also contain health benefits, so after the second season, you can harvest the entire plant.

Step 5: Safely Preparing Nettles

For culinary use, you always have to cook nettles thoroughly. This is how you deactivate the sting and remove the toxins. It only takes about a minute of boiling to achieve this. If you don't eat the leaves immediately, they will last in a bag in the fridge for around three days.

Leaves can be dried in a bag or air-dried. You should leave them for at least two weeks but store them before they start to turn brown. Properly dried leaves lose their sting because the tiny hairs fall off, so always check for this. Another good trick is to pop them into a food processor before freezing them, eliminating any "stringiness" in the leaves.

HERBAL REMEDIES WITHOUT THE STING

You can use nettle leaves the same way you would spinach or sauté them in a bit of butter. The roots and leaves can be used dried or fresh to make tea, and if you want to add some extra fiber, boil the stems too.

You can make a decoction or add leaves to a poultice for joint pain. If you feel brave, you can use the traditional method of rubbing fresh leaves onto the skin near the pain. The heat works like many of the deep heat creams available. During allergy season, try taking a few drops of tincture every day. You can also infuse water or vinegar with nettles to give your hair a nettles rinse for extra shine.

Personally, I don't fancy rubbing that much heat on my joints after a day in the garden, but my nettle salve works wonders. The next herbal plant also has the ability to make us cry but not in the same way as nettles! You probably have plenty in your pantry, but onions are something we can grow ourselves and save money on!

19

ONION

Allium Cepa

Onions have been around for over 7,000 years and can grow in the wild on all continents. According to some, before New York was nicknamed the Big Apple, people would call it the Big Onion. This is because you can peel back so many layers before reaching the center. Aside from their popularity in the kitchen, onions are packed with health benefits.

THE NUTRIENT-DENSE ONION

Onions are a vegetable worth loving due to their nutrient-dense nature; they offer high levels of nutrients while being low in calories. In particular, onions are a rich source of vitamin C and B vitamins such as B6 and B9, which act as antioxidants in the body. Moreover, onions are a great source of potassium, a nutrient that many people tend to lack in their diet.

Increasing your onion intake can help with inflammation, to reduce cholesterol levels, and lower the risk of heart disease. Red onions are especially beneficial for this and protect the body from cancers like colorectal, ovarian, and lung cancers. It may also help to manage diabetes symptoms and improve bone strength. With antibacterial properties, onions can slow down the growth of bacteria like E. coli. With fiber and prebiotics, onions can also improve gut health and aid in digestion.

STARTING WITH ONION SEEDS OR SETS?

Onion sets are very small, mature onions that tend to have a higher success rate because they can cope with a light freeze. They look like small bulbs, and you should choose sets that are about ¾ inch in diameter. There are various times to plant seeds and sets, but you should select an area with full sun and where the soil has no rocks or debris to disturb growth.

Step 1: Onions Like Nutrient-Rich Soil

You can plant sets directly outdoors once the temperature is consistently above 28°F. Depending on how many sets you want to grow, you can dig a trench or holes. The space should be around 2 inches deep, adding about an inch of compost before placing the bulb with the pointy end up. Cover with roughly 1 inch of soil. Be sure to keep 5 or 6 inches of space between sets.

If you are planting onion seeds, ensure the soil temperature has reached a minimum of 50°F and plant just ¼ inch under the soil. I would always add compost to the soil because onions are heavy feeders. If you prefer, you can start seeds indoors six weeks before you want to transplant them outdoors (with the same spacing).

Onions can also be planted in the fall. Just be sure to give them around five weeks in warmer temperatures. This way, they have time to establish and then go dormant for winter.

Step 2: Treat Onions Like a Leafy Veg

A good set of healthy foliage is a sign of a healthy root! I like surrounding my onions with mulch to help with weeds and water retention. In most cases, rainwater will be enough, but as the temperatures heat up, they will need about 1 inch of water per week. Giving them plenty of water will sweeten the flavor.

Step 3: Homesteading for No Waste

Rather than chucking onion tips on the compost heap, you can grow a new plant from your kitchen scraps. Save the bottom inch of the onion and let it dry out for up to 24 hours. Insert a cocktail stick (like a toothpick, but longer) into the onion. Choose a glass or small bowl and add water. Place the onion bottom side down so that it sits in the water. Leave the onion in a sunny area for 3 or 4 days. You will see the roots sprouting. Then you can move the onion to a container and cover it with 1 or 2 inches of soil. Water it straight away.

Step 4: The Trick to Harvesting Onions

In the middle of summer, you will notice that the leaves start to turn yellow and droop. Bend the leaves back and loosen the soil around the base. This will help the onions to ripen and dry. By late summer, you can gently pull up the onions. Gently is key because bruising can encourage rot, especially when you store them.

Step 5: Curing Onions for Storage

The weather should still be dry, so leave onions out for a few days to cure. Then you can either braid the dried foliage together to hang it or, if you cut it off when you harvested it, hang it in a mesh bag. The onions that smell sweeter should be eaten first because they have a high water content. Stronger onions will store better for longer. Don't store your onions in the fridge because of the dampness.

For long-term storage, you can chop the onions and place them in a bag to be frozen. They can be kept in the freezer for up to 12 months!

NON-CULINARY USES OF ONIONS

If you aren't keen on eating raw onion but need to get rid of a toothache, you can grate an onion to squeeze out the juice. The onion juice can be rubbed onto gums and straight onto the skin for problems like boils, bruises, wounds, sprains, bites, and fungal skin conditions.

I can't believe how effective a cut onion can be for coughs, colds, and congestion. All you need to do is take half of a freshly cut onion and place it near your pillow overnight. Yes, the room smells "ripe" the next day, but your symptoms will be greatly relieved.

If your nose can't "stomach" this pungent odor, don't worry - the next herbal remedy smells far better than raw onion!

20

PASSIONFLOWER

Passiflora Incarnata

Passionflowers are simply stunning to have in any garden. Native to South America, they now grow in parts of America and Europe. Folklore says that the passionflower got its name because the corona looks like the crown of thorns worn by Jesus during the crucifixion.

CAN PASSIONFLOWER HELP YOU?

One of the primary uses of passionflower is to help with stress, anxiety, and related disorders. The plant extract can increase dopamine levels in the brain. By reducing anxiety, it is also thought that passionflower can help with sleep problems too.

Passionflower might help to reduce stomach ulcers, relieve burns, and treat hemorrhoids. It may also be used to help manage the symptoms of ADHD, heart rhythm problems, and menopause, but more research is needed to confirm this.

HOW TO ADD THIS STUNNER TO YOUR GARDEN

It looks like an exotic plant that requires much effort to grow. However, passionflower is an excellent choice for homesteaders because it's such a multi-purpose plant. Aside from the beauty and fun of growing passionflower, the fruit, flowers, and leaves are edible.

Step 1: Testing Seed Viability

Passionflower seeds are a little tricky to germinate, which can be disappointing when your germination rate is less than you had hoped. It can take months for seeds to germinate, so if you aren't that successful, you may feel you lost a season.

To prevent this, nick the seeds with a knife and soak them in water overnight. Viable seeds will sink while the infertile ones float on top. Plant your seeds ½ inch into the soil and, for greater success, use a heating mat or place the containers in a plastic bag. Check the containers daily and gently mist them to ensure the soil doesn't dry out. With this extra heat, your seeds should germinate within 20 days.

You do want to make sure you have at least two passionflower seedlings. This will encourage pollination later on. Without two plants, it will be a lot harder for fruit to grow.

Step 2: Transplanting and Caring for Passionflower

The seedlings will be ready to harden off and transplant outdoors when they are a few inches tall. Passionflowers are heavy feeders, so add compost to the soil, whether in a container or directly into the garden.

For zones 6 to 10, your plant should do well outside. Otherwise, it might be safer to transplant it into containers so that you can bring the plant indoors over the winter months. For both scenarios, include a support when transplanting. Passionflowers are climbers with impressive vines. Water passionflowers as soon as you transplant them. As they love full sun, be sure to water them well twice one week as they grow and every other day if they are in containers.

People prune passionflowers mainly to control their growth, especially if it is being kept as an indoor plant. The ideal time for this is in early spring or winter. You should still make sure that dead stems are cut back if they don't die back to the ground.

Step 3: A Unique Way of Propagating Passionflower

You can take a stem that is at least 4 to 6 inches long and cut just below a node. Cut off the bottom leaves and dip the end of the stem in honey to help the roots develop. Plant the cutting 1 inch into the soil and lightly water. Place a plastic bag over it, ensuring the remaining leaves don't touch the plastic. The roots should develop in a few weeks as long as the cutting stays warm and moist.

A fun way to propagate passionflower is by tip layering the vine. Find a vine tip that is long and healthy. Cut the leaves back and make a little dip in the soil nearby. Look for the smooth side of the vine and place this side facing down in the soil. Put some soil over the vine. If the vine doesn't stay in place, put a small rock or stone on top of the soil. By next spring, you should have a new passionflower vine!

Step 4: What to Harvest and When

Flowers tend to appear from spring onward. Cut the flower's stem in the morning once the dew has dried.

Try to choose the flowers that are wide open. Pick off the sepals, stamens, and pistils from the center of the flower and trim off the stem.

When a vine reaches its third season, it is mature enough to produce fruit. Depending on the variety and the climate, fruit can appear from March to November. You don't have to harvest passionflower fruit. When ripe, they will fall off the vine.

Harvest leaves as needed, or use the leaves from the stems you have harvested for the flowers or during pruning.

Step 5: Different Storage Methods

It's easier to lay leaves flat on a tray and leave them in a well-ventilated area until they snap. Wash the fruit and pat it dry with a paper towel. Fruit will last in the fridge for one week as long as you don't put it in a plastic bag. Leave the fruit out of the fridge for a few days if it isn't quite ripe enough.

Flowers can be used fresh or dried. Flowers take 3 to 5 days to completely dry when in a single layer and left in a sunny spot.

THE BEST WAY AND TIME TO TAKE PASSIONFLOWER

Fresh leaves can be eaten raw in salads or cooked like spinach, and they make nice additions to quiches, curries, and pasta dishes. The dried leaves are ideal for making teas and can also be added to tinctures. The flowers, whether fresh or dried, are also great for infusions and tinctures. Add drops of the tincture to water and juice. Use all of the parts to infuse the oil for skin problems or use them in a poultice.

Like kava, I would take passionflower at night because of its relaxing properties. Avoid passionflower if you are pregnant or breastfeeding, and be extra careful if you take any sedatives. There may also be interactions with blood thinning medications.

I came across passionflower by luck, really. I chose it because of the incredible flowers and because I wanted to add height to my garden. I confess I like to use the flowers to show off a little in the kitchen as well as take advantage of the health benefits.

The next plant is a favorite among Indigenous Americans and is particularly useful in the bedroom!

21

PATCHOULI

Pogostemon Cablin

It never ceases to amaze me how one plant family can have so many varieties; this is especially true of mint. Patchouli is another member of the mint family with stems that can reach 5 feet. The plant produces plenty of pink-white flowers that provide a wonderful scent. It's also a herb rich in history. When Tutankhamun's tomb was opened, there were gallons of oil inside, and during the hippie era, patchouli was literally worth its weight in gold!

THE MEDICINAL USES OF PATCHOULI

The essential oils in patchouli can release the happy hormones serotonin and dopamine. This may help to reduce anxiety and improve mood. Some active ingredients in patchouli can act as a sedative to help with sleep. It's popular in beauty products because of its ability to help regenerate skin cells, and with antibacterial properties, it may help treat acne.

As with so many of our herbs, patchouli has anti-inflammatory properties. It could help with digestion, improve the absorption of nutrients, and give you more energy. Another use for patchouli is as an aphrodisiac, as it may stimulate the production of estrogen and testosterone, boosting men's and women's libido.

GROWING PATCHOULI WHEN YOU DON'T LIVE IN WARM OR TROPICAL CLIMATES

Patchouli is a perennial herb native to Asia. It does well in hardiness zones 9 to 11, but as it copes with shade, it's also a good choice for a houseplant. If you are growing it as a houseplant, you can start the seeds anytime!

Step 1: Take Care With the Seeds

Patchouli seeds are quite fragile, so treat them with care. You can start seeds indoors around six weeks before the last frost or find a sunny spot in your garden with some shade and well-drained soil. Sprinkle seeds onto the soil and gently push them slightly into it. For the next 1 to 3 weeks, spray the seeds to keep the soil moist.

Step 2: Transplanting Your Seedlings and Care

When your seedlings have their second set of leaves, they are ready to be transplanted into larger containers. If you are planting in the garden, keep a distance of 24 inches. I use a spoon to carefully lift the soil around the seedlings to not damage the roots. At this point, if you are growing them indoors, you can start hardening them off. They will be happy outdoors when there are 4 to 6 hours of sun daily. Try to find a spot with shade in the afternoon because direct sunlight might be too much.

Check the moisture of the soil every couple of days. Waterlogged soil isn't good for patchouli. Although you don't want to neglect watering, the plant will bounce back quite well if you see signs of wilting. During the growing season, pinch off the tips to encourage more flowers.

Step 3: Propagating in the Fall

Fall is the ideal time to take a cutting. Choose a young, green stem that has at least one node. This stem will typically be at least 2 or 3 inches long. Place your cuttings in a jar and fill it with water until just below the lowest set of leaves. The cutting can be planted in soil when the roots grow to around 1 inch long. Water them daily with a mister.

Step 4: The Harvesting Scent Test

You can harvest leaves 5 to 6 months after planting the seeds. A couple of tricks will let you know when to start harvesting the leaves. First, the stems will turn brown, and you will also notice that the plant starts to give off its unique rich musky smell.

You can harvest leaves when needed or take a larger harvest but never more than a third of the plant at a time. Again, like most plants, it's best to harvest in the morning after the dew has dried.

You can harvest flowers, but the main benefits are in the leaves.

Step 5: How to Save Patchouli Leaves

Drying leaves gives you the most possibilities. Lay leaves out so that they are in a single layer. The leaves should be left out of direct sunlight in a well-ventilated area until completely dried. Do the snap test before storing the leaves in an airtight container. Even the slightest moisture can cause mold.

HOW TO TAKE PATCHOULI

Most of the benefits from patchouli come from inhalation. This can be done through potpourri and scented candles. I would add some flowers to the potpourri. This may also help keep insects out of the home! Infused oil for massages, hair, and skin is another way to inhale the benefits.

The leaves are edible, so you can also make teas and tinctures from fresh or dried leaves. You can try adding them to different foods as a seasoning, or with a large enough harvest, eat them as a vegetable.

Most homestead gardeners develop a sensitive nose, and just the scent of a plant is enough to calm them. Walking past a health food shop and inhaling, you almost feel healthy! Patchouli has that same effect. The earthy, sweet, and spicy smell of patchouli in the garden and in the home is marvelous. I can't help but stop and smell the patchouli in my garden.

The following chapter will look at another plant typically grown for its leaves. It's also a favorite of mine because of its multiple uses and because it grows wild all around me.

22

PLANTAIN

Plantago Major

Before we go into the details, it's worth explaining the difference between the tropical plant and the perennial herb that pops up in many of our lawns!! The tropical plantain is related to the banana, and the plantain we are interested in is easily grown in US hardiness zones 3 to 9.

WHY THE BROADLEAF PLANTAIN IS HEALTHY

The plant's leaves contain a slippery mucilage that doesn't sound very attractive but does wonders for healing wounds. It's a great plant to put on insect bites and stings, rashes caused by allergies, hives, burns, cuts, and scrapes. If you have chosen to grow nettles, keeping plantain close by for accidental stings is a good idea.

With its anti-inflammatory properties, plantain can also be used internally for coughs, sinusitis, and respiratory conditions like chronic bronchitis and to relieve gut inflammation symptoms and ulcers.

WHO CAN GROW THIS WEED-LIKE HERB

This plant has large, broad-shaped leaves that grow close to the ground and a long leafless stem that produces flowers. It's perfectly safe to grow around pets and children, and because it loves all types of soil, anyone can grow it.

Step 1: Finding Your Seeds

Plantain is found so easily in the wild that you may not even have to buy the seeds. If you spot this plant, get permission before entering someone's land. They will probably be grateful if you dig up the whole plant! The roots are shallow, so either dig around the base to transplant the entire plant or carefully pick some flowers and place them in a paper bag.

Choose an area in your garden that is away from other plants to help control its spread. Dig a hole slightly larger than the root ball you have dug up and plant it. The seeds are tiny and do better with a period of cold stratification. If you want to collect the seeds, just shake the flowers in your hand, and you will see them. Place them in a plastic bag with some moist soil in your fridge for 4 to 6 weeks. Sprinkle the seeds onto your garden soil and then sprinkle a thin layer of soil on top.

Step 2: Let the Plantain Be!

Plantain needs little water, except in dry climates with no rainwater, you may not need to water it at all. More or less, in its ideal zones, a plant will need 1 inch of water per week. There is definitely no need to feed your plantain plant either!

Step 3: The Step You Might Want to Skip

Each plantain plant can produce a whopping 14,000 seeds. Moreover, although the seeds won't germinate until the following spring, they can remain viable in the soil for up to 60 years. My best advice would be to collect some seeds from the long stems that produce dozens of small flowers in case your existing plant doesn't self-seed, which is unlikely. Seeds are also easily blown in the wind, so look for signs of germination in other areas of your garden.

Step 4: Which Leaves Should You Harvest

Plantain is a very forgiving plant and is happy for you to harvest leaves throughout the whole growing season, before or after flowering. You should look for the inner leaves and cut them off at the base. The outer leaves are a little tougher.

The roots also contain medicinal properties. If you are pulling up plants to control the spread, wash off the roots to make the most of them too.

Step 5: Fresh Is Best With Plantain

Because you have a nice prolonged harvest, use fresh leaves as often as possible. The leaves can be dried in bundles hung upside down or individually on racks in a dark place. Thoroughly dried leaves will snap. Roots can also be used fresh or dried, and again, to dry them, leave them in a well-ventilated area until they snap. As they are thin, this shouldn't take more than a few days to 1 week, depending on your humidity.

WHAT TO DO WITH ALL YOUR PLANTAIN

Fresh leaves are ideal for a poultice because of the healing liquid we discussed. Mash the leaves with a pestle and mortar, adding a little water to make a paste. Apply this directly to the wound for anywhere from 10 minutes to overnight. This poultice may also help remove splinters and shards of glass.

Use the early harvested leaves for tinctures, but dried leaves can also be used for tinctures when there isn't a harvest. The young leaves are also lovely in a salad and cooked in stews and soups. Plantain tea is slightly bitter, but you can add it to other hot and cold drinks for an alternative flavor.

I like to treat my plantains like overly enthusiastic puppies. Of course, they need love and attention, but they also need rules and control for our relationship to be mutually beneficial!

In the next chapter, we will look at a popular herbal plant to help with sexual health, but like many, there is more than one benefit from saw palmetto!

23

SAW PALMETTO

Serenoa Repens

Palm trees are synonymous with exotic holidays and lying on a beach with the warm sun on your face. To have a little bit of that in your garden warms the heart! But palm trees aren't practical for most of us. So, the next best, and healthier, is saw palmetto. This resembles a palm tree but is a hardier shrub, tolerating different conditions.

THE TROPICAL PLANT TO HELP TABOO SUBJECTS

It's the saw palmetto fruit that contains medicinal benefits, and it's also a fruit favored by animals like raccoons, opossums, wild pigs, and even black bears. Berries are rich in flavonoids, fatty acids, sterols (for cell structure), and carbohydrates.

Starting with the general uses, saw palmetto may help with colds, coughs, sore throats, migraines, and asthma. It may also help combat stress! There is some evidence to show that it might treat male hair loss and chronic pelvic pain.

Though some people use it to increase their libido, it is often used to help with benign prostatic hyperplasia (BPH), an enlarged prostate. Research has been mixed, but one meta-analysis examined 1,080 people with BPH. After six months of daily use, urinary flow improved, although there was no change in prostate size (Cai et al., 2020).

BRINGING A TOUCH OF FLORIDA TO YOUR HOMESTEAD GARDEN

The Indigenous people of Florida ate fruit from saw palmetto, though the plant doesn't produce the most delicious berries. The fan-shaped leaves grow close to the ground, and the plant gets its name from the sharp spines along the edges of the leaf stalks.

Step 1: Check Your Temperatures

Saw palmetto is native to zones eight and above, so ideally, you need temperatures of 25°F to 97°F. Below this, you will need a decent amount of space in your greenhouse. It can grow up to 10 feet tall and anywhere from 4 to 10 feet wide. Collect some berries for the following season if you know someone with a saw palmetto plant.

The seeds are slow to germinate, so it's best to nick the seeds and soak them in water for around 24 hours. If you want to grow it as a hardy shrub, choose a location with partial shade. You can also start seeds in containers where they will be happy for a few years. Spring is the best time to plant the seeds when temperatures are around 60°F. Plant the seed ½ an inch to 1 inch into the soil and keep the soil moist with a mister. It can take a month before you see sprouts.

Step 2: What Saw Palmetto Needs to Fruit

Aside from taking care with the temperature, saw palmetto only needs good watering once a week if there is no rainfall. After 2 or 3 years, you will need to transplant the saw palmetto into a larger container or to its permanent home, again taking care that there is some partial shade. Don't be surprised if it's not until between years 3 and 6 before your plant has berries.

You only need to prune dead parts of the plant or stems that have fruited.

Step 3: To Propagate or Not?

A plant in the right conditions can easily live for 20 years; some species live for hundreds of years. As this plant won't propagate from roots or cuttings, you will need to grow new plants from seeds. With such a long lifespan, you will have plenty of time to do this!

Step 4: Harvesting the Fruit

Harvesting the berries can be a painstaking task made much simpler with a decent set of gloves and well-covered arms. I would stick to old clothes in case the spikes catch on them. The berries are found under the leaves and can stain your clothes if you aren't careful.

Ripe berries will be between the size of an olive and a cherry tomato and be a deep, rich, purple color. They are normally ripe from August through to November. Pick the berries with your hands but have a bucket nearby to avoid having to lift the leaves too many times.

Step 5: What's Next for Your Berries?

Berries can be stored in airtight containers in a dark place for a couple of days. Much longer, and they start to spoil. When harvested, berries contain around 66 percent water, and considering how quickly they spoil, it's hard to dry these berries naturally. You will need to use a dehydrator or oven set below 140°F, turning them occasionally until they are crispy between the fingers. When dried, they will last for up to 2 years.

You can also freeze the berries whole. After washing them, make sure they are completely dry so that they retain their shape. Place them in freezer bags and remove as much air as possible without squishing the berries. This way, there is less risk of freezer burn. They will last in the freezer for around three months.

WHAT CAN YOU DO WITH SAW PALMETTO

It's worth trying raw berries for their unique flavor. You will get hints of sweetness, pepper, and perhaps even blue cheese. I recommend nibbling the berries because the seed is quite large, allowing your taste buds to get used to the flavor.

Teas and tinctures are suitable for daily use. If you are making a tincture, it might take a little longer, depending on the strength of your alcohol. I leave mine for up to 3 months and shake it once or twice daily for the first two weeks.

If you have dried some berries, you can grind them into a powder and add the powder to other drinks and desserts if you like the flavor. I also add a little powder to butter icing to decorate cakes instead of colorants.

You should stop taking saw palmetto if you notice any side effects like dizziness, upset stomach, headache, or fatigue. As the extract can influence hormones, you should check with your doctor if you have breast or prostate cancer.

My berries have all come from a kind friend, as I haven't planted my own saw palmetto yet. I would love to hear how you get on and any tips and tricks you have. I will be with you as soon as I can find some space in my garden!

Continuing with the theme of berries, we will move on to buckthorn. While there are many types of buckthorn, it's sea buckthorn that catches our medicinal interest.

24

SEA BUCKTHORN

Hippophae Rhamnoides

Sea buckthorn isn't a true buckthorn but an incredibly hardy shrub that can survive the harshest of winters, even temperatures as low as -45°F. It's another plant where the name is more interesting in Latin. Hippophae comes from hippo, meaning horse, and phae meaning shining. One of the traditional uses was to feed sea buckthorn leaves to horses to improve their weight and coat.

THE HEALTH BENEFITS OF SEA BUCKTHORN

We use leaves, flowers, and fruit to make herbal remedies. The leaves have high levels of antioxidants, amino acids, and minerals. Along with the flowers, the leaves are used to help with arthritis, stomach ulcers, skin rashes and to lower blood pressure and cholesterol. They can help to keep blood vessels healthy and, as a good source of vitamins, boost the immune system.

The berries may loosen phlegm, treat asthma, and improve eye health. They can also support a healthy heart and possibly improve cognitive function. Sea buckthorn berries might improve acne and heal different kinds of skin wounds, including burns, eczema, and dermatitis. You might notice sea buckthorn as an ingredient in anti-aging products.

GROWING SEA BUCKTHORN IN 5 STEPS

Not only can this plant tolerate low temperatures, but it is also not fussy about the soil type. As long as the soil is well-drained and there is plenty of sun, you won't need to worry about where you plant it. You do need to make sure you grow both a male and a female plant to make sure there is pollination and fruit, which grows on the female plant.

Step 1: Experimenting With Seed Germination

Throughout the growing season, you can try different ways to start your seeds but planting them straight in the ground isn't the best way to ensure success. Trying different methods at different times can give you a better idea of the best germination methods for your climate. With a piece of medium grit sandpaper, scrape the outside of the seeds, a process called scarifying. Strange fact, this process mimics the seeds passing through a bird's digestive system and encourages germination! The seeds can then be planted in the fall or very early spring.

Another option is to scarify the seeds and then cold-stratify them for 30 to 90 days in the fridge with some moist soil in a plastic bag. They can then be planted outdoors in the spring or soaked for two days in water and then planted. Only sprinkle soil over the seeds because they really do need light to sprout. Some people even take the plastic bag out of the fridge and leave it in the sunlight until the seeds germinate.

Step 2: A Tip to Improve Growth

If you don't have sandy soil, mixing some sand into the soil before planting is a good idea. This will allow for better drainage. More than this, full sunlight is crucial for the female plant to bear fruit. Another thing to consider is the space sea buckthorn needs. The roots spread wide, and the plant forms runners, so ideally, it will have a 9-foot space to grow into. Sea buckthorn is highly drought tolerant, so you only need to water it if you are growing it in a container.

Female sea buckthorns should be pruned every other year, but it might be enough to trim the stems back when you harvest the fruits. Male plants only need to be pruned every few years but never take more than half the shoots so there is enough pollen for the female plant. In both cases, you should still cut back dead stems. If the plant gets too dense, thin stems out to improve air circulation.

Step 3: Using Hardwood Cuttings for Propagation

You can propagate from a cutting in the fall or spring, but it should be a cutting from the previous year's growth. Cut about 6 inches of the brown stem and place this in a jar with water so that around two-thirds of the cutting is in the water. Until an inch of roots has formed, change the water daily. The cutting can be planted in a container and kept indoors for two months while the roots properly develop and then be transplanted outside.

Step 4: Looking for the Brightest Berries

From August onward, the berries will start to turn a bright orange color. This is a sign that the berries are ripe enough to pick. There are thorns on sea buckthorn, so you will want to get those gloves out again. To harvest the berries individually, you can use a fork to separate them from the branches or cut the whole stems back. As the weeks pass, you may notice that you can shake the branches, and the berries fall off.

Step 5: Storing Your Berries

Fresh sea buckthorn berries will last in the fridge for up to a month. They can also be frozen whole or puréed and then frozen. Leaves and flowers can be spread out on a tray to air-dry and then stored in air-tight containers. They can also be crushed or ground into a powder.

To air-dry the berries, you first need to dip them in a liter of boiling water with a teaspoon of baking soda. This will help preserve the health benefits. Dry them off with a paper towel and then leave them on a tray. It takes about a month to dry them fully. In the oven, it will take approximately 3 hours at 100°F.

Another way to preserve the fruit is to fill a jar with berries and add boiling water. Seal the jar tightly and leave it to cool down completely. Once cool, it can be kept in the fridge or a pantry for up to a year.

"BERRI-LICIOUS" WAYS TO USE SEA BUCKTHORN

Use your leaves and flowers for tinctures and teas, but the most fun is had with the berries. First, the berries can be juiced (my favorite way to start the day), made into a jam, or added to baked goods like cakes, pies, ice creams, and sauces. Like saw palmetto berries, you can eat them raw but expect a somewhat tart, tangy taste. The flavor pairs well with other fruits like apples, melon, and mango.

Other uses are to infuse the oil for topical use and add it to beeswax for a salve. If you made juice, save the pulp. This makes fantastic skin products. Try blitzing the dried pulp with rolled oats until you have a powder. The powder can be added straight to your bath or mixed with salt or baking soda and made into a paste with a bit of water for a skin rub.

Sticking with herbal remedies for the skin, witch hazel is one of the most popular plant remedies added to skin and acne products, so popular that many of us wouldn't think twice about growing the plant. Nevertheless, it does more than radiate skin!

25

WITCH HAZEL

Hamamelis Virginiana

Witch hazel is a favorite of mine because my shrub flowers in November when nothing else is blooming. It gives the garden a little color to contrast with the typical winter doldrums. Witch hazels are actually a genus of plants called Hamamelis, meaning together with fruit. This is because the plants produce flowers at the same time as the fruit from the previous year matures. The name has nothing to do with witches. Instead, it comes from the old English word wice, meaning bendable. Hazel might be because the plants were used as divining rods, much like hazel twigs were.

THE ACTIVE INGREDIENTS IN WITCH HAZEL

The main active compounds in witch hazel are tannins and polyphenols. Tannins have antioxidant properties but can also help fight inflammation and have antibacterial effects. This is why witch hazel is so prevalent in skin treatments. It can reduce bacteria on the skin, reduce redness and inflammation, and soak up excess oil. Overall, skin tone is improved. Polyphenols may reduce signs of premature aging!

Many don't realize that witch hazel can also be consumed, although I strongly discourage ingesting the essential oil because of its strength. Tea, for example, may help with colds, fever, and upset stomach, and the antioxidants may also act as an anti-inflammatory and help prevent some cancers. However, there isn't enough evidence to prove this.

GROWING THE RIGHT TYPE OF WITCH HAZEL

There are four main types of witch hazel. The most commonly grown in the States is American witch hazel which grows in hardiness zones 4 to 8, as does Ozark witch hazel. Japanese and Chinese witch hazels prefer zones 5 to 8. American witch hazel blooms from October to December and the other three from January to March, possibly April, so bear this in mind when it comes to harvesting.

Step 1: The Cold Process

Witch hazel seeds are notoriously slow to germinate and can take up to 2 years to sprout without intervention. We can speed up the process by exposing them to heat, cold, and heat again. Place freshly harvested seeds in a plastic bag with moist soil and leave the bag somewhere that is around 85°F for 2 to 3 months. After this, put the bag in the fridge for another three months making sure the soil stays moist. Finally, you can plant the seeds in starter pots and leave them in a warm, shady area that is approximately 75°F.

Doing this should encourage germination within around three months. Gradually harden the seedlings off from the end of spring to summer.

Step 2: Choosing a Permanent Home for Witch Hazel

Plants prefer full sun unless they are in hotter climates where partial shade will help them. Once the seedlings have been hardened off, you can plant them in your garden or keep them in containers for a few years. Eventually, they must be planted into the soil for adequate growth space.

The soil should be kept moist, and when the plants are young, this is especially important. It's a good idea to add a layer of mulch to help retain moisture, and if you keep the plant in a container, keep a closer eye on the soil moisture.

Pruning isn't necessary, but you may need to cut the stems back after they have bloomed in order to control growth. Depending on the type, witch hazel can grow to be 15 to 20 feet tall and wide! Pruning will also encourage more flowers the following year. Whatever you do, don't prune witch hazel in winter, as it will bleed and dry out.

Step 3: Speeding Up the Process Again

It can be six years from seed to plant before you see signs of flowering. Growing witch hazel from a cutting can get you fruit and flowers faster. Take 3 or 4 cuttings, each around 4 inches long, and pinch off all the leaves except the top set. Place all the cuttings in a container with fresh soil and cover the cuttings in a plastic bag.

Keep the container in a cool place, around 60°F, for two months for the roots to develop. Then transplant each cutting to its own container. Maintain the same cool temperature until the following spring when the cutting can be hardened off and planted outdoors.

Step 4: How to Harvest Witch Hazel

You can cut thin twigs and their leaves at any time during the growing season, but spring is when the sap is strongest. Cut twigs below the nodes and strip the leaves. Cut the twigs into 1-inch sticks. If the twigs are thicker, you can use a knife to scrape the bark off.

The medicinal benefits are in the leaves and twigs. Try to leave flowers on the plant. They really brighten up a winter garden and, the following year, will produce fruit. The fruit is necessary for seeds, whether you harvest them or let pollinators do their jobs.

Step 5: Drying Techniques for Witch Hazel

The leaves should be dried indoors where there is heat and good airflow. After three days, check for crumbliness, but it could take one week to completely dry. Twigs and bark can be dried in the sun but are best dried indoors. The more air they can get, the faster they will dry. When dry, they will snap rather than bend. You can store the dried parts in jars or paper bags.

BEST USES FOR WITCH HAZEL

For topical use, you can make a salve or decoction. Decoctions are handy because you can apply the liquid directly to your skin, the same with a salve. I combine aloe vera with witch hazel for a salve. If you make a witch hazel tincture, dilute a couple of tablespoons in half a cup of water before using it.

You can add some fresh or dried bark to your homemade candles for inhalation. If you are fortunate to have an open fire, add some twigs and enjoy the smell. Use fresh leaves to mash them up into a paste for a poultice.

Teas and tinctures can be taken orally but with care. Start with a weaker tea and diluted tinctures; you can increase the strength if there are no reactions.

Our last herb on the list is one that is more often associated with mental health. Nevertheless, as our mental and physical health are so closely related, valerian can support our overall well-being.

26

VALERIAN

Valeriana Officinalis

I envy people who can go to bed and fall asleep straight away, or who wake up at night and are asleep again in minutes. My brain has other ideas, but I found that valerian made a big difference in the quantity and quality of sleep I got, which in turn, improved my days!

WHAT THE EXPERTS TELL US ABOUT VALERIAN

The use of valerian goes back to Hippocrates, who used the root to treat insomnia. Today, it is sometimes called nature's Valium because of its calming properties.

Compounds in valerian include valepotriates, monoterpenes, and flavonoids, which may account for its effect on sleep and relaxation. It can also lower gamma-aminobutyric acid (GABA), a chemical messenger that regulates nerve impulses in the nervous system.

One study showed that people who took valerian 30 minutes before going to bed fell asleep faster, slept for longer, and woke up fewer times during the night compared with those taking a placebo (Palmieri et al., 2017). A more recent study supported the use of valerian for anxiety. Valerian root extract taken 1 hour before bed significantly reduced anxiety symptoms in 39 people (Tammadon et al., 2021). Valerian may also help those with OCD, hyperactivity, and difficulty concentrating.

GROWING VALERIAN IN 5 STEPS

Another reason to love valerian is that it is a perennial that dies back in winter and returns to life in spring, so it's safe to plant outdoors in cold climates.

Step 1: Keeping It Simple With Valerian Seeds

You can start seeds indoors around four weeks before the last frost, but because they are so easy to grow, you can save some work and plant them directly in your garden. Choose an area with well-drained soil and preferably full sun in the morning with some shade in the afternoon. Sow the seeds ½ an inch deep with a space of at least 11 inches. When planted in spring, the seeds should germinate within 2 to 3 weeks.

Step 2: Making Sure Valerian Doesn't Become Invasive

In terms of water, valerian needs consistently moist soil, so don't let the top layer dry out. You may only have to water in summer without enough rainfall. It is essential to prune the spent flowers. Valerian will reseed and spread, so keeping on top of the flowers will help to stop it from invading your garden. The flowers have a lovely scent, so you can even add them to a vase in your home.

Step 3: Propagating Valerian Roots

In the second year, your plant should reach about 18 inches tall. By then, it will have developed extensive roots. You can dig up a valerian plant, separate the root ball and replant both halves. You can also take a young cutting to propagate, but it's often best to divide the roots to stop them from becoming over-cramped. Propagate valerian in spring so there is enough time for the roots to develop before winter.

Step 4: Harvesting Roots at Their Peak

The most health benefits in valerian roots are found in spring and fall. If you divide the roots for propagation in spring, you can take half of the roots and only replant the other half. In the fall, you can dig up a whole plant to harvest. Cut back the stems and wash the roots off. Like propagating, you should wait until the second year to harvest the roots.

Step 5: Watch Out for the Smell

Unlike the lovely fragrant flowers, the roots have quite a stench to them. Because of this, I don't dry them indoors, and most certainly don't stink up my oven. You can tie the roots into bundles and hang them or lay them out on a tray to dry the roots. In both cases, they need good airflow and about two weeks to dry fully. The roots can be stored whole or ground into a powder. Dried roots will last for 2 or 3 years.

TAKING CARE WITH THE RIGHT USE OF VALERIAN

Fresh and dry roots are used for tea, decoctions, and tinctures, but that's not the only way to take in the calming effects. A salve and a massage oil are extremely relaxing, and you may find it helps with rashes and bruises too. You can also add the roots to a bath or foot soak.

As a mild sedative, take care when using valerian. It's another one of the herbs that I stick to for evening use. You should also be careful if you take sedatives or medications broken down by the liver. Avoid valerian if you are pregnant or breastfeeding because there isn't enough research. Valerian should only be used for a short time. After six weeks, you should gradually reduce your intake.

Throughout the chapters, we have looked at a number of ways to use your herbs, but in our final chapter, there will be 17 simple recipes that can inspire you to do more with your harvest.

27

17 MORE SIMPLE RECIPES FROM SOUPS TO SALVES

I love cooking, but I confess that I am a bit of a free spirit in the kitchen. I might find a recipe with the main ingredients I like, but I rarely stick to the amounts, and I will more often chuck in a bit of this or that to see what happens. The amounts I have included are only rough guides, and I hope you will experiment to make sure your taste buds are happy. The same can be said for non-culinary creations. Start with lower amounts if you are worried about allergic reactions, and then feel free to use more plant parts or brew/infuse for longer.

1. Nettle Pesto

- 5 cups of raw nettle leaves
- 2 cups of fresh basil leaves

- ½ cup of parmesan
- 2 tablespoons of lemon juice
- 2–3 garlic cloves
- Extra virgin olive oil

Put all of your ingredients in a food processor except the olive oil. Pulse the ingredients for a few seconds. Gradually add the olive oil while blending until you get the pesto consistency you like.

2. Marigold Fritters

The following amounts are for two people, but you can multiply them depending on how many portions you want to make.

- 10–12 fresh marigold flowers
- 4 tablespoons of flour
- 3 tablespoons of milk
- 1 egg
- ½ teaspoon of red chili powder
- ½ teaspoon of ginseng powder
- Salt and pepper to taste
- Oil for frying

Mix the red chili powder, ginseng, salt, and pepper into the flour. Make a space in the middle of the flour and crack in the egg. Mix the egg and flour, slowly adding the milk until you have a batter. I use a fork to prevent lumps! Dip the marigolds into the batter so they are well-covered, and add to a pan with hot oil. Fry until they are golden brown all over.

3. Roasted Vegetables With Dill and Onion

- Veggies of your choice (potatoes, carrots, zucchini, and mushrooms are my favorites)
- 2 medium-sized onions
- 3–4 cloves of garlic
- Small bunch of fresh dill
- 3–4 tablespoons of oil

Because there is a big difference in cooking time between some of these veggies, I start by making sure they are cut to a similar size and boil the potatoes and carrots until partially cooked. Peel the onions and cut them into chunks (like orange segments). Peel the garlic and cut it in half. Add all the veggies to a bowl with the oil and mix until they are covered well. Pour them into a backing tray. Roughly chop the dill and sprinkle on top. Bake in the oven for 30 minutes at 395°F, and turn occasionally.

4. Sea Buckthorn and Bergamot Jam

- ¾ cup of grams of sea buckthorn berries
- ¾ cup of grams of thinly sliced bergamot
- 2/3 cup of water
- Sugar (the amount depends)

Place the fruit in a saucepan and add the water. Bring it to a boil and cook for about 10 minutes. You can use a masher to help break up the sea buckthorn berries to get the juice. Strain the mixture using a fine mesh sieve and use a spoon to press the pulp, making sure all the juice is out. Pour the juice into a measuring jug. Use a ratio of juice and sugar of 1:1.5 Add the sugar and juice to a saucepan and boil until it reaches 235°F. Transfer into a mason jar and leave to cool.

5. Cinnamon and Apple Pinwheels

- 1 sheet of shortcrust pastry
- 2–3 cooking apples
- A handful of sultanas (optional)
- Cinnamon powder
- 1 egg

Peel the apples and dice them into small cubes. Roll the pastry out flat and generously sprinkle it with the diced apples and sultanas. Then sprinkle the cinnamon powder on top. Roll up the pastry and cut it into 1-inch slices. Lay the pinwheels on a sheet of parchment paper and brush with a beaten egg. Cook in the oven at 350°F for 20 to 25 minutes. You can dust the cooked pinwheels with brown sugar or icing sugar if you want.

6. Dandelion and Chocolate Milkshake

- 1 cup of cold milk
- 1 heaped teaspoon of cacao powder (cocoa is an alternative)
- 1 heaped teaspoon of dandelion powder
- ½ teaspoon of cinnamon (optional)

Add all of the ingredients to a blender and mix well. If you want a thicker shake, reduce the amount of milk and add a large spoonful of vanilla or chocolate ice cream.

7. Lady Fern Fiddlehead and Pork Stir-Fry

- 2 cups of pork strips
- 1–2 cups of fiddleheads
- 1 small onion
- 2–3 cloves of garlic
- ¼ cup of chicken stock or bone broth
- Soy sauce
- White wine

- ½ teaspoon of sugar
- Salt
- Pepper
- Oil
- Optional extras: green beans, mushrooms, baby sweetcorn

Begin by marinating the pork in the soy sauce, sugar, and salt for the time that suits you. Heat some oil in a frying pan and fry off the pork slices. You may need to do this in batches. Once all the pork is cooked, leave it to one side. Use the same pan with a splash more oil to fry the fiddleheads for 2 to 3 minutes. Add the vegetables to the pork. Chop the onions and garlic. Start frying the onions, and once soft, add the garlic. After a minute, add the pork and vegetables. Pour in the wine and stock, a splash more soy sauce, and the pepper. Stir for a couple of minutes and serve!

8. Lemon Balm Popsicles

- 2 cups of lemon balm leaves
- 6 cups of water

This is so simple the kids will love helping you make these healthy popsicles. All you need to do is simmer the leaves in water for 20 to 30 minutes, longer if you want the popsicles to be stronger. You can also add different flowers to the decoction if you have leftover harvest and not just those from this list. Lavender will give your popsicles a nice purple color!

9. Gotu Kola Soup

- 3 cups of freshly picked gotu kola
- 2 cups of coconut milk
- 1 cup of water
- 1 teaspoon of fresh ginger (or ½ teaspoon of powder)
- 2 cloves of garlic
- 1 teaspoon of lemon juice
- Salt and pepper

Finely chop the gotu kola leaves, ginger, and garlic. Add all of the ingredients to a saucepan and bring to boil. Turn the temperature down so the soup can simmer for 20 minutes. Use a hand blender to get the consistency you want or serve it as it is. A popular Sri Lankan dish adds rice. Other alternatives include cucumber and chicken.

10. Kava and Patchouli Bath Salts

- 3 cups of Epsom salts
- 1 cup of Himalayan pink salt (optional)
- 1 tablespoon of dried kava

- 1 tablespoon of dried patchouli

There are two ways to make bath salts, you can infuse the oil and add a few drops to the combined salts or you can crumble the plant parts between your fingers and add the parts to your salts. You can have lots of fun making your own bath salts, especially with dried flower petals.

11. Hibiscus and Mint Iced Tea

- 4 cups of water
- 1 cup of dried hibiscus flowers
- ⅔ cup of fresh mint leaves

Add the hibiscus and mint to boiling water and leave it to steep for 5 to 10 minutes. You can substitute mint for lemon balm if you prefer. The tea can be served warm or over ice.

12. Goldenseal Hot Toddy

- 2 cups of brandy
- ½ cup of fresh goldenseal roots
- ½ cup of fresh goldenseal leaves
- Orange juice
- Lemon slice
- Honey

Begin by making a tincture with the brandy and goldenseal. To make the hot toddy, boil some water. Pour two fingers of orange juice into a cup, then add a teaspoon of honey and 2 or 3 teaspoons of the tincture. Top off with hot water and a slice of lemon.

13. Ginseng Cookies

- 1 cup of flour
- ½ cup of sugar
- ½ cup of golden syrup
- ⅓ cup of butter
- 1 teaspoon of ground ginseng
- 1 teaspoon of baking soda
- ½ teaspoon of ground ginger (optional)

Sift the flour, ginseng, baking soda, and ginger if you want. Mix in the sugar and then begin to rub the butter in with your fingers. Mix in the golden syrup so that you end up with a dough. Separate the mixture into small balls and squash them flat. Spread them out on a piece of parchment paper and bake at 350°F for 10 to 15 minutes.

14. Passionflower Curd

- 10–15 passionflower fruit pods
- ⅔ cup of sugar

- 4 large egg yolks
- 6 tablespoons of butter
- 1 teaspoon of lemon zest (optional)
- A pinch of salt

Add a heat-proof bowl to a saucepan of water (2 inches of water is enough). Bring to the boil and then turn down the heat to simmer. Add all of your ingredients to the double boiler, except for the butter. Continuously mix the ingredients—this is crucial if you don't want your egg yolks to curdle. When the sauce becomes thick, carefully remove the bowl. Add the butter in small cubes and continue to mix. Pour the mixture into a container and cover. Use your passionflower curd the same way you would lemon curd.

15. Witch Hazel Skin Toner

- 1 cup of witch hazel bark
- Vodka
- ¼ cup of apple cider vinegar
- ½ cup of distilled water

Start by making a tincture with the vodka and witch hazel, leaving it for 2 to 4 weeks, and shaking it daily if possible. Strain the witch hazel from the tincture and add 1/4 to a 1/2 of a cup of apple cider vinegar. Add around ½ a cup of distilled water or enough to fill your jar. Shake before you use it. If you have arnica, you can add this to the tincture too.

16. Onion and Hibiscus Syrup

- 1 onion
- 1 cup of hibiscus flowers
- ½ cup of honey
- 1 lemon

The traditional recipe uses sugar but this is a healthier version. Finely chop the onion and add the pieces to a jar. Roughly chop the hibiscus flowers and add them to the jar, stirring so that they are well mixed. Add the juice of a lemon and the honey. Seal the lid on tight and give it a good shake. Leave the jar in a warm place for a day. Strain the syrup and keep it in the fridge.

17. Eucalyptus and Plantain Salve

- 2 cups of coconut oil
- 1 cup of plantain leaves
- 1 cup of eucalyptus leaves
- 6 tablespoons of beeswax

In a double boiler (a heat-proof jar in a saucepan of water), add the oil, plantain leaves, and eucalyptus leaves. Let the oil simmer for 3 hours or until the oil smells of the herbs. Strain the oil and add it back to the double boiler. Gradually add in the beeswax until it completely melts. Dip a teaspoon in the mixture and put it in the freezer for a few minutes. Test the consistency of the cooled salve, adding more oil or beeswax if necessary. I would also save a few spoons of the oil before adding the beeswax to use in the bath or mixed with salt for a face scrub.

Just like with growing and using herbs, the ingredients in these recipes are flexible and can be customized to suit your preferences. These recipes serve as inspiration for how you can incorporate herbal remedies into your routine. If you decide to try them out or experiment with additional ingredients, I would be delighted to hear about your experience.

CONCLUSION

Before we go any further, did you download the full color Companion Guide with a picture of every herb in this book? If you didn't see it when you started this book, it is the page right before the introduction. We have discussed 25 amazing herbs and I know you want to see what they look like!

Many non-homesteaders will ask me why I go to "such lengths" to grow my own pharmacy. Regardless of the gardening philosophy you choose to follow, there is no doubt that patience is required. Today, in such a busy world, it's true that it might be easier to rush down to the pharmacy at the first sign of illness, but only in the short term.

Growing herbs for medicinal purposes far outweighs the benefits of relying on pharmaceuticals and grocery stores. The most beautiful irony of homestead herbs is that you can actually reduce the need for medication by growing your own.

Homestead gardening gets you outdoors, where you are active and taking in the fresh air, which is revitalizing after a long day at work. Growing things in your garden helps you to slow down and appreciate the simpler things in life, and at the same time, there is plenty of bending, stretching, and carrying things.

This simple practice does wonders for your mental health. Just 10 to 15 minutes in the garden, taking care of plants, and seeing the results gives you an amazing boost of confidence. Not only can you grow something from a seed, but you can also take those first steps toward becoming self-sufficient. You really do have moments of super confidence and the feeling you can do anything!

Whether you choose a fast-growing culinary herb or a perennial shrub that takes a little longer, you know that the efforts you make now will last a lifetime. As soon as your children catch the homestead gardening bug, you have just passed an incredibly beneficial skill on to future generations. Remember the adage, "Give a man a fish, you feed him for a day. Teach a man to fish, you feed him for a lifetime!"

Twenty-five plants are a lot to start in one go, and even as an experienced homesteader, I wouldn't do it. Each season, I add one or two new plants if I have the space, and this is a good rule of thumb to stick to. Again, aim for an annual and a perennial so that you have something fast-growing and something that will require less maintenance and last longer. And don't forget the importance of native plants for your own confidence and for the pollinators.

A final tip that I would give when selecting your first or next herb is to choose a herbal plant for each area of the body. Berries are full of antioxidants and can help with overall well-being. Then, try to select a plant for your relaxation, one for the skin, and one for aches and pains.

Another thing that I have heard time and time again is people wondering what to do with their harvest, and I feel that this is another way of nature showing her irony. So often, we don't think that anything will grow, and just a few months later, there is a big harvest, and you aren't sure what to do with it all.

Watch out for this type of thing with extreme weather changes. One year I planted my chili seeds confidently, and then nothing happened. That year had been extremely hot, even too hot for chili, and nothing happened. Surprisingly, in September, my plants started to flower, and I had around 40 chilies overnight. If in doubt, dry, freeze, or give to others. Never waste!

The first & second books, *Homesteader Herbal Handbook* and *Forget the Pharmacy – Grow Your Own Medicine,* were so popular; I can't thank everyone enough. They both made it to the Amazon Best Sellers list – Something I never even considered possible. I promise that your enthusiasm is what keeps me going when it comes to sharing my gardening experience. Considering the different soil conditions, climate, seed quality, harvest, and storage methods, I think it is crucial that we continue to share our herbal homestead experiences. We are all capable of learning more!

Would You Help Me?

On that note, I am asking everyone if they could take a minute or two to leave a review on Amazon. Naturally, I learn a lot from your feedback but Amazon reviews do so much more than just help me as an author.

Many of us are experiencing increasing costs in all areas of our life, and even more of us are suffering from the stressful lives we lead. By sharing your opinions, others get to see that they have the means to take control of their own health and well-being and that of their families.

I want to say good luck and in the past, I would have. But you have 5 simple steps to grow 25 more herbal remedies, so I will leave you hoping that you have fun! And don't forget you can email me anytime at hello@ homesteadmindset.com and share your stories!

REFERENCES

Andújar, J. R. (2020). *Apoptotic activities of Mediterranean plants.* Science Direct. https://www.sciencedirect.com/topics/agricultural-and-biological-sciences/lemon-balm

Cai, T., Cui, Y., Gao, Z., Yu, S., Li, Q., & Zhou, Z. (2020, April 10). *Comparison of* Serenoa repens *with tamsulosin in the treatment of benign prostatic hyperplasia: A systematic review and meta-analysis.* Sage Journals. https://journals.sagepub.com/doi/10.1177/1557988320905407

Günthardt, B. F., Hollender, J., Hungerbühler, K., Scheringer, M., & Bucheli, T. D. (2018, June 26). Comprehensive toxic plants–Phytotoxins database and its application in assessing aquatic micropollution potential. *Journal of Agricultural and Food Chemistry, 66*(29), 7577–7588. https://doi.org/10.1021/acs.jafc.8b01639

Herbal History: Roots of Western herbalism. (2021, February 1). Herbal Academy. https://theherbalacademy.com/herbal-history/

James River Association. (2021, May 11). *Native, non-native, invasive—and dandelions!* https://thejamesriver.org/native-non-native-inva sive-and-dandelions/

Kianbakht, S., Khalighi-Sigaroodi, F., & Dabaghian, F. H. (2013). *Improved glycemic control in patients with advanced type 2 diabetes mellitus taking Urtica dioica leaf extract: A randomized double-blind placebo-controlled clinical trial.* National Library of Medicine. https://pubmed.ncbi.nlm.nih.gov/24273930/Improved glycemic control in patients with advanced type 2 diabetes mellitus taking Urtica dioica leaf extract: a randomized double-blind placebo-controlled clinical trial

Lee, S., & Rhee, D. (2017, January 24). *Effects of ginseng on stress-related depression, anxiety, and the hypothalamic-pituitary-adrenal axis.* National Library of Medicine. https://www.ncbi.nlm.nih.gov/pmc/articles/PMC5628357/

Morabito, C. (2022, February 28). *Why health-care costs are rising in the U.S. more than anywhere else*. CNBC. https://www.cnbc.com/2022/02/28/why-health-care-costs-are-rising-in-the-us-more-than-anywhere-else-.html

National Health Portal India. (2016, May 20). *Introduction and importance of medicinal plants and herbs*. https://www.nhp.gov.in/introduction-and-importance-of-medicinal-plants-and-herbs_mtl

Palmieri, G., Contaldi, P., & Fogliame, G. (2017, May 26). *Evaluation of effectiveness and safety of a herbal compound in primary insomnia symptoms and sleep disturbances not related to medical or psychiatric causes.* National Library of Medicine. https://www.ncbi.nlm.nih.gov/pmc/articles/PMC5457154/

Pareek, A., Suthar, M., Rathore, G. S., & Bansal, V. (2011, June). *Feverfew (Tanacetum parthenium L.): A systematic review*. National Library of Medicine. https://www.ncbi.nlm.nih.gov/pmc/articles/PMC3210009/

Soumyanath, A., Zhong, Y., Henson, E., Wadsworth, T., Bishop, J., Gold, B. G., & Quinn, J. F. (2012, February 15). *Centella asiatica* extract improves behavioral deficits in a mouse model of Alzheimer's disease: Investigation of a possible mechanism of action. *International Journal of Alzheimer's Disease, 2012*. https://doi.org/10.1155/2012/381974

Statista. (2022, March 9). *Average spices & culinary herbs prices per unit in the United States 2014–2027*. https://www.statista.com/forecasts/1291280/average-spices-and-culinary-herbs-prices-per-unit-in-the-united-states

Tammadon, M. R., Nobahar, M., Hydarinia-Naieni, Z., Ebrahimian, A., Ghorbani, R., & Vafaei, A. A. (2021, March 31). *The effects of valerian on sleep quality, depression, and state anxiety in hemodialysis patients: A randomized, double-blind, crossover clinical trial.* National Library of Medicine. https://www.ncbi.nlm.nih.gov/pmc/articles/PMC8077445/

University of Melbourne. (2013, May 13). *World first clinical trial supports use of Kava to treat anxiety*. ScienceDaily. https://www.sciencedaily.com/releases/2013/05/130513095750.htm

Printed in Great Britain
by Amazon

32573692R00116